River Characters

Deep Thoughts and Shallow Stories about Fly Fishing

By Walter J. Wiese

BWO Books

BWO Books

Portions of this book were previously published in the magazine *River Hills Traveler* and on the website *Rocky Mtn Fly*.

Designed by Walter J. Wiese

Manufactured in the United States of America

ISBN 978-0692349991

About the Author

Walter J. Wiese is owner and outfitter of Yellowstone Country Fly Fishing Guide Service and Head Guide at Parks' Fly Shop, both located in Gardiner, Montana. His writing has appeared in *American Angler, Fly Rod & Reel, Flyfishing & Tying Journal*, and many other publications. He was the 2001 recipient of the Buck Rogers Memorial Award for excellence in outdoor writing. He has written one previous book, *Yellowstone Country Flies*, a fly tying manual.

Walter has guided in southwest Montana and Yellowstone National Park since 2001 and has lived on the doorstep of the park since 2006.

Visit Walter at http://www.montanafishing.guide.

Table of Contents

Cold Day in the Shop

"Boooonniiiieeee," I called as I rose from my tying station, scissors in one hand and fragment of beef jerky in the other. Boonie the Shop Dog woke immediately and jumped to his feet like a puppy, knowing from past experience what was about to happen. He trotted over to the rack of neoprene waders, where no one ever goes, and hid behind the sun-faded bootfoot waders hanging there. As he trotted, that lovely, lovely white tail caught a ray of sunshine that had broken temporarily through the low overcast, and seemed to glow.

Eventually, the beef jerky won out, and Boonie emerged from hiding long enough for me to snip a clump of white hair. Forty seconds later I was securing a perfectly stacked wing on my Skykomish Sunrise. There wasn't a single steelhead within five hundred miles, but I could plan. Besides, steelhead flies were more entertaining than another damn dozen foam beetles for the shop's fly bins.

Planning for future trips and entertaining yourself are what slow days in the shop are all about. At the fly shop where I work, in early June, when the Yellowstone fifty yards away is still running filthy and the overcast might mean rain or snow down here in the valley but definitely means snow up high, there's a lot of time for both. On occasion we'll see only two or three customers all day, and one will just want to use the bathroom.

After the Skykomish Sunrise, I moved on to Bombers. I didn't have to chase down the dog for materials to tie them, and since the only fish I've ever caught on steelhead dries are cutthroat out of pocketwater creeks and rainbows in the Yellowstone during the Salmonfly hatch, I figured they might actually prove useful. As I tied in the tail of the first, Phil, one of the other shop guys, came back in, fighting to shut the door behind him against the blast of north wind, clutching his third cup of gas station coffee of the morning.

Boonie emerged from hiding again, looking as cute and innocent as a twelve-year-old Border Collie/Blue Heeler mix can manage. "More treats?" he seemed to say.

Phil only patted him on the head, but he looked over at me like he was going to offer me a treat instead. He stuck his hand in his jacket pocket, grinning.

"I don't want any," I said.

He pulled his hand out of his pocket and, voila, revealed a Super Ball. "I found it in the street," he said. He bounced it to me.

I forgot about tying flies. I go through a Bomber about once every three years, so bouncing a rubber ball across the shop was far more important. We proceeded to bounce the ball to each other across the shop for the next twenty minutes, pausing once to direct a Japanese tourist looking for fleece to the camping store down the street. The woman looked shell-shocked. Clearly, it was not 38 degrees and spitting rain in Tokyo. We only ended our game because an errant bounce sent the ball flying into the office/warehouse in back, into which the fly shop's guide trip clients must carry rations when they go back into the stock room try on rental equipment. The ball will be found by archaeologists 3000 years from now excavating a fly shop tentatively dated to the 1970s. Only the fossilized lost foam hoppers they'll find in the ductwork will suggest their dating might be incorrect by a few decades.

Fun ended, Phil announced he was taking lunch. Boonie went with him, willing to brave the elements on the off chance there'd be a piece of cheese or smoked whitefish in the offing.

What to do, what to do? The cane rod on the rack behind the counter caught my eye. It's a 1970 Orvis Battenkill that never sold, and probably never will. It's never been fished, but it's sure been cast. There was no way I was going outside, but with a handful of old fly line we use to practice our needle knots and the rod's tip section, I could practice my accuracy casting indoors. The framed 8x10 picture of the nine and a half pound brown a client caught a few years ago was as good a target as any, and it is a straight shot from the picture to the far wall of the store, a good distance over which to practice my double hauls.

This practice got old in a hurry. Without a reel, it was too easy to shoot the entire line across the room to puddle against the picture. Oh well. On the plus side, I'd noticed a few almost empty fly bins on the display while I was casting, including the blond CDC & Elk Caddis that represent the White Miller caddis that would soon hatch on the Firehole. Time to earn my wages.

I got half a dozen done before Phil and the dog returned from lunch. Boonie was still licking his chops. Phil had his latest kitsch creation, a giant Trude made of yarn, paintbrush fibers, and pipe cleaners tied on a shark hook. A fly for catching tourists instead of trout. So far this season he'd sold two similar flies. The new one was still missing hackle, so it looked like he wanted to be productive for a while as well.

I just wanted lunch.

After I ate, I returned to tying, keeping at it until I had two dozen caddis on the table in front of me, enough to fill the bin through at least one good caddis day. Then it was back to tying for myself. Tired of steelhead flies I might never use and not interested in puzzling my way through a tourist-trap fly like Phil was working on, I decided to make something that might be useful at some point in the near future. The only question was what that might be.

"Did you go take a look at the river when you went to get lunch?" Phil said.

"No, didn't see the point. Why?"

"It must be below freezing up high. There river's cleared out a bit—there's probably eight inches of viz. Want to go out after work?"

Did I really have to answer that? It looked like giant stonefly nymphs were what I needed to tie. Keeping ourselves busy on a slow day in the shop with games and busywork is okay. Fishing—even on a cold, wet day when a handful of fish caught by dredging big nasty nymphs right on the bottom was all we could expect—is a lot better than that.

As It Should Be

"Are you sure this thing will float with two people in it?" I said. My cousin Jack and I were standing on a boat ramp on the shore of a lake whose name I'm not allowed to mention, getting ready to shove off after loading fly rods, cooler, and a couple boxes of carp flies. The stern of the boat was still on dry land, for good reason. The boat was one of those cheap Bass Pro Shops hard plastic things that looks like the bastard child of a cracker box and a soap dish, and it had been used hard. At that time Jack usually fished alone, so to launch the relatively heavy boat he would simply push it off the roof of his Toyota Tercel and drag it down concrete boat ramps to the water. The heavier end of the boat, the end with the battery and motor, would grind against the concrete the hardest.

Jack fished *a lot*.

There was a hole in the stern below the waterline big enough for me to stick three fingers into. "Sure, it'll float. The stern just dips a bit. The thing is full of Styrofoam, you know."

At the time, Jack was out of work and getting by on bargain store white bread, stocker trout, and all the panfish he could catch. Consequently, he was a skinny guy. This is an adjective that has never been applied to me. The boat was only nine feet long, and had a weight capacity of 450 pounds, presumably including water. Jack's reassurances were not very convincing.

Well, I figured, the lake was warm.

On the other hand, it was also filthy muddy and full of... something. As the electric motor hummed us along towards the great carp gathering spot Jack knew about, enormous bow wakes would surge from the weed beds near the bank towards deeper water. I hoped they were big carp, but being a science fiction fan, I had visions of H. P. Lovecraft's tentacled creations heading towards deep water not out of fear, but to set traps for us.

After three quarters of a mile, Jack turned us down a narrow creek arm where the water was noticeably clearer than it had been in the main lake. I started to wonder if the 0X leader I'd tied on was going to be too heavy. Then I looked at the leader Jack was using, a level strand of 20lb test, and figured I was okay.

A hundred yards down the channel, around the first bend, a footbridge appeared. Jack cut the motor to slow and told me to get ready. "Get your feet set. The first shot is the best, and they'll spook if they feel ripples from you moving your feet."

7

I smiled and figured he was joking, though the channel was indeed smooth as glass. The banks were higher here than those in the main lake, and in some spots the trees almost met above us, giving the channel a humid, primeval atmosphere, broken only by the whoosh of cars on the highway invisible through the trees and the chatter and gasps of families standing on the footbridge, looking down at our quarry. "There wouldn't be that many people there if there weren't a lot of carp," Jack said, and again cautioned me to get set.

He scowled at me as I moved my feet one last time, after he cut the motor. It was hard not to shuffle my feet. There were perhaps twenty carp hovering near the bridge pilings, all but motionless. Shadows loomed over the fish, people gawking at the colossal fish. The bridge led to a popular suburban nature center, and though it was now against the rules to feed fish from the bridge, it had once been popular. The carp remembered, and thus gathered whenever the nature center was busy. We were fishing on a Saturday afternoon on a nice day in September, when lots of people felt the urge to go for a stroll outside. Lots of people meant lots of carp looking for handouts.

Inertia carried the boat to within thirty feet of the bridge. I was in perfect casting position, in sight of more sheer poundage of fish than I'd seen outside of a hatchery. My fly probably would have worked in a hatchery, come to think of it. I was using a giant ball of white egg yarn lashed to a #8 streamer hook, soaked "Magic Sauce" dry fly floatant, the best big bug floatant on the market, to match the hatch, the bread that some people certainly still threw for the carp.

Okay, to be honest, we had a loaf of bread, too. It was against the rules to feed the fish from the bridge, but we weren't on the bridge, and chumming for non-game fish is perfectly legal in Missouri. The bread was of the same brand of cheap white bread that Jack was living on at the time. Indeed, over the course of the afternoon he ate about as much as the carp did.

But the chum was only for after the carp got spooky and sank down out of sight into the muck. Now, I had a clear shot at fish near the surface, and I took it. My big white fly settled a foot in front of a group of three carp, all between about eight and fourteen pounds. Average fish for this lake. The fly was about as dense as a piece of bread, and settled like one, to hover in the surface film in an amorphous blob.

A carp awoke from its nap and finned to the fly. It came lazily, and rose with agonizing slowness. It sucked in the fly, and as soon as it started down, I set. Then the fish was off to the races, or would have been if I didn't immediately palm down on my spool, testing the 0X tippet almost to its limits. The fight was not flashy, but by the time I brought the carp beside the boat, far up the creek, where the fish had run, my right arm was quivering. The fish weighed twelve pounds, the largest fish of any species I'd ever landed up to that point, on the fly or otherwise, and still in the top five.

After we shuffled past each other, my cousin taking his place in the bow and me in the stern, on the motor (I noticed immediately that the boat was down significantly at the stern), my cousin got ready for his shot. I had used my eight weight, a rod suited to the task. He was the one who had the carp fishing on this lake dialed. He had caught eight in one afternoon a few weeks past. To up the ante, he chose to fish a 7'6" four-weight. I told him he was insane.

The fish were spookier now, and many had scattered as my fish thrashed. A handful still hovered near the bridge, however, in more sheltered spots, up among the bridge pilings and near the logs piled against the bank, deposited there in some long-forgotten flood. It took several casts, but Jack finally interested one that hovered up in the shadows deep under the bridge. A moment after he set, the fish dove for the bridge pilings. Jack put what I thought was way too much pressure on the fish, making good use of the rope-like twenty pound test he was using, bending the little rod all the way to the cork. The fish turned from the logs, but shot off down the creek channel towards the main body of the lake, with occasional lunges towards the weed beds.

Jack screamed at me to follow, and after a moment of fumbling I popped the motor to full power and gave chase. The water filling the stern slowed us, and line peeled off Jack's reel. It was a cheap reel, and he didn't have an inch of backing on it. People were gathering on the bridge now, pointing. They had probably done the same thing when I was hooked up, but I had been far too busy to notice.

Soon we were far enough away that the gawkers lost their show, but the fish was beginning to tire, and though its lunges towards the weeds were still its best chance at freedom, it now came up and rolled on the surface at times. The boils it made gave credence to my Lovecraftian fantasies during the ride across the lake. The fish had been indistinct beneath the bridge;

now its true size was revealed. My carp was its younger brother, maybe infant brother. It could have eaten the entire loaf of chumming bread as a nice midnight snack.

I don't remember anything Jack and I said when we saw how big his fish really was, but I'm sure we screamed loudly enough that the people on the bridge could hear. I'm also sure we said some things to cause the tourists to cover their kids' ears.

At last Jack brought the fish up beside the boat. We each got a hand on it and dragged it in for pictures. The carp was so big that estimating its weight was at best an educated guess. Based on the terrible pictures I snapped, we estimate it went twenty pounds, maybe even more. Jack has size fourteen feet, and one snapshot I took shows one of his shoes next to the fish's head, heel beside its snout and toes barely past its gills.

The fish was big enough that Jack couldn't even hold it at arm's length, in the traditional perspective-destroying grip and grin pose. It still looked huge.

We eventually got the carp back in the lake and made our way back to the bridge. The crowd was still there, but they departed when it became clear that another fish would not soon be forthcoming. As I had quickly learned when I first tried for a carp and failed utterly at it, carp are not stupid, and after having not one but two of their brethren dragged away, the rest sank to the bottom and scattered. It was time to break out the bread.

As afternoon faded and the light got flat, we cruised at the motor's slowest possible speed up and down the creek channel, looking for the bronze flashes of carp feeding against the banks. When we spotted a fish, the man on the motor would toss slices of bread towards the fish like frisbies. Most often, the bread was ignored. When, once in a great while, a fish would tilt upward to suck in the watery morsels, the angler would drop a cast in the fish's path. Now the carp were more cautious, however, and save for a single six-pounder that tilted up like a trout towards my fly but flashed away with a boil at the last moment, none paid our offerings the slightest attention. Jack tried creeping a nymph along the bottom beneath the bridge for a few minutes, but one of the sunfish that usually hovered among the carp picking up their crumbs was his only reward.

At last, when the light was far gone, we broke down our gear and turned for home. The battery was starting to go, and there were enough snags between the creek and the ramp that to return in total darkness was unsafe. We said little as we made our slow way back across the lake. A quarter of the way home, a night fisherman in the distance turned on his boat lights, attracting both insects and fish. Jack's boat lacked lights as well as a sound hull, and its electric motor was silent and not powerful enough to leave a wake. Though we passed less than two hundred yards from the other boat, I saw no sign that the angler in it noticed us. Only the boils of carp far larger than the one Jack had landed darting for deep water suggested that anything at all noticed us, which is as it should be.

First Day

Yellowstone River, April 25, 2006

Later in the season, I wouldn't have called the Yellowstone fishable. After a four day warm spell that turned the river to concrete with runoff, on the 24th it had turned suddenly cold and blustery, with snow above the 6000-foot level in Yellowstone and on the mountain passes Interstate 90 crosses between Livingston and Missoula. I knew about the snow because I had driven through it hours before, making the long drive east to Gardiner, Montana after my last quarter of grad school and last month of solitary steelheading in northwest Washington State. I thought the Yellowstone would be just a touch off-color, with big trout slashing streamers as though they hadn't seen a baitfish before. I felt a visceral need for this to be true.

13

But that warm spell hung around like a bad hangover, and the river had at best a foot of visibility even immediately below the Gardner's mouth, though this smaller river flowed almost clear. Away from its clear tributary, the Yellowstone was a filthy mess. The trout would be shivering on the bottom, unwilling to move more than a couple inches in the cold, cloudy water.

Richard said Dailey Lake would be fishing, and he was probably right, but Dailey Lake was thirty miles back towards Livingston and inhabited only by hatchery-bred quasi-trout, perch, and walleye, and it was already late afternoon. With the cold, the fishing everywhere would shut off once the direct sunlight was off the water. Any activity would likely be happening now, either here on the Yellowstone or on the lake. I was standing right next to the Yellowstone, so that's where I fished, even if the conditions were far from right.

To be honest, I probably would have fished the Yellowstone if it had been so blown out that trees had been careening downstream like canoes piloted by drunks. After my last trip to the Skagit, back in Washington, I needed to fly fish for trout that bad.

•

My six-weight felt like a toy after the giant spey rod I'd fished exclusively through the winter and early spring, Boy's First Fly Rod or an accessory for Fly Fisher Barbie, maybe. It would not feel this light again that season, since a six-weight is about as heavy as I typically fish for trout, but that afternoon I handled it more delicately than I needed to, marveling at the lightness in its tip, at the reel less than five inches in diameter. The 3X tippet and 4X dropper were more miraculous yet, spider silk after the 12lb Maxima and 0X fluorocarbon I'd fished all winter. I hadn't fished a tippet weaker than 2X since October, when I'd landed three steelies in an hour and a half on the North Fork of the Stillaguamish using 4X. I have fond memories of that afternoon. It was well past now, though, and it remained to be seen if I'd snap the lighter tippets the first time I had a strike, forgetting for a moment that I was trying to drive home a #12 nymph twenty feet away rather than a big Intruder eighty feet away.

I started with a giant tunghead rubberleg Copper John, a refugee from one of my steelhead boxes, above a Bead, Hare, and Copper, one of those nymphs that can be just about anything and whose stocky profile and heavy copper rib would help it stand out in the murk. A commercial fly tier I knew had fished the same stretch just before the warm spell, and had caught thirty in a couple hours fishing the nymph (which he invented) beneath a stonefly (another of his patterns), with all the hits coming on the Bead, Hare, and Copper, an endorsement if ever there was one. I expected my results would be similar. The Mother's Day caddis were just waiting, down in the gravel and among the cobbles and boulders, and the Hare & Copper does a fair jo matching their pupae. If a fish ate the Copper John I wouldn't complain, but I really chose it to serve as weight.

Over the next twenty minutes, I lost two Bead, Hare, and Coppers and began a musical chairs routine with the top fly, switching between various stoneflies, Copper Johns, and even a Thunder Egg, another steelhead refugee. I kept the Bead, Hare, and Copper on the bottom, still hopeful that a fish could

15

see it in the dirty water. Nothing else happened as I worked my way downriver, still following the rhythms of swinging a fly downriver for steel even though fishing upstream would have made more sense with the nymphs.

Then I came to a patch of water where the topography of the steep bank, lack of overhanging trees, and a momentary and minuscule break in the overcast allowed a beam of sunlight to fall on a twenty-foot run, whereas the water closer to the Gardner's mouth had been in shadow. In happier weather perhaps a few early Mother's Day caddis would have been hatching from this short stretch already, prompted by the sunlight and warmer water from the Gardner River fooling them into thinking it was time to hatch already, but today there were none. There were trout, however, three of them. I caught two little rainbows, the larger stretching all of nine inches. The third was a cutt-bow that flopped free as I brought my rod vertical to lift the fish from the river.

It was a start, but just that. While in the dog days I'd happily hit tiny mountain creeks in pursuit of high country brookies and cutts no bigger than those little rainbows, they weren't much of a way to start the year. Not necessarily because of their size, but because of their size in relation to the waters in which they lived. The Yellowstone through Gardiner has an average fish size smaller than elsewhere on the river, a function of its precipitous gradient here perhaps, but an average trout is still eleven or twelve inches long.

I'd come to Gardiner that year uncertain of what I'd be doing after the season ended, if I'd stay in Gardiner and attempt to eke out a living editing brochures and web copy for local businesses, if I'd pursue an internship, or if a job far from the river would suck me in with the promise of several times the income I could expect to make on the Yellowstone or near it. Just guiding in the summer, with no promise of a winter job, was getting untenable. With my future after the end of the season unclear, I needed a symbol, something to tell me that I was where I should be. Getting an average fish, one not too small nor too large, would do the job, would be a symbol confirming that I'd made the right decision in coming to Gardiner so early in the year, rather than trying to get some temp job in Bellingham, Seattle, or back in the Midwest, or even chucking the guiding thing and trying to find a real job immediately. I'd had a signal that signified it was time to leave Washington, but without another to close the circuit I'd created in my mind, I might second-guess myself, think that perhaps I'd made a mistake in leaving Bellingham, or should have done something else with my spring or perhaps my life.

•

Bellingham, Washington, Late March and April 2006

Late March and April went like this: I'd wake up, and if it wasn't forecast to be too windy or too bright, and it wasn't a weekend when the hordes would be out, I'd go thrash the Sauk or Skagit, without result save for many lost flies, marabous and articulated leeches and Intruders that sank on their heavy steelhead irons to hang in what seemed like every rock. In hindsight I should have hung up the Spey rod at the end of February, when a friend and I had landed a pair of bright native steelhead, mine a fish so recently ascended from saltwater that not a hint of color showed on her sides, not the faintest blush of a rainbow's stripe. She was only silver and gunmetal gray, like the weather that day.

On days when the weather or my inclinations kept me in bed, I'd wake at 9:00 or so, drink a giant cup of coffee, and furiously tie flies all day. By the time I packed up my tying gear for the move to Montana, I had a couple thousand tied. I've never been a speedy tier, so five dozen would take most of the day. Afterwards I'd flip through magazines and web sites, searching for more, looking for patterns I could tweak, turn into my own, turn into something that more precisely matched the *Flavilinea* in Soda Butte Creek. I rationalized all this by telling myself that I'd made tying my job, for March and April. Meanwhile, any time I left the house it seemed like a HELP WANTED sign glared at me, told me that my long preparation for Montana was a mistake, told me that I should be starting up the ladder. Which ladder was an open question. I should at least have been building up a bankroll to help sustain me through the next winter, which would be my first without at least the modest stipend of a grad student teaching the basic composition classes that all the real professors despised, to say nothing of the freshmen who had to take them.

And I was still trying for another steelhead, a big one, the kind of fish that ate flies larger than the first two rainbows I caught in my first hour back in Gardiner. Steelhead remained an enigma to me: in two falls, two winters, and one full spring in coastal Washington, I'd managed to land nine. This was nine better than many beginning steelheaders manage over the same amount of time, but I was just barely getting my double-spey cast down to the point where I could shoot line, and barely learning to see the steelhead lies amid the riffles, the water different from that enjoyed by the cutthroats, browns, brookies and 'bows that I could now read well. Soon enough I'd go, leaving the steelhead behind for the indefinite future, returning to water I loved, whose characters from runoff to the first tendrils of winter's long cold slumber I'd experienced enough to have a feel for the broad rhythms, if the specifics often enough surprised me.

Yet I'd also be going into something new, going to Gardiner thinking I might stay for good, this time, rather than leaving come near the end of the tourist season for other jobs or more graduate school and serfdom as a part-time composition instructor. And I was scared by this. A template lay open for me: get a normal job in Seattle or even working for one of the less heinous government bureaucracies, make lots of money, and fish on vacations and the weekends. Though an MA in English with a concentration in writing creative nonfiction is no ticket to fortunes, this template would have been easy enough to follow to the letter: even weeks after graduation several of my fellow grad students were stepping onto the beginning of this path, with something else filling the spot in my vision occupied by fishing.

So I was uncertain about my decision to leave the relatively green pastures of western Washington for the uncertainty of Gardiner, or rather the uncertainty of what would come after the upcoming guiding season, and my second thoughts on not getting a job in the months after graduation was only a symptom. Then I went steelheading one more time, with the Skagit and Sauk at optimal flows and, the word on the street had it, the entire system chockfull of steelhead.

The first run where I stopped was already occupied by a fly angler. Not really a problem, as I had another couple runs on the other side of the river in mind, as backup options. It was early enough in the morning that I figured these runs would be empty long enough for me to fish them.

I was wrong. A boat full of bait fishermen, competition of a sort I seldom encounter in Montana, arrived at the first run just as I did. Who arrived first was an open question, but a neighborly thing for the boatman to do would have been to shove on down to the next run, leaving the slow, bank-bound angler (me) a run to himself. Boat anglers can fish every run on the river, after all. Instead the oarsman kept back-rowing, allowing the angler in the bow to probe every nook and cranny in the pool with his roe sack. It paid off handsomely, with a twelve- or fourteen-pounder, a bright, bright fish though I was fishing the Sauk far upstream of its confluence with the Skagit, half again as far from tidewater as the run I'd fished on the magic day in late February. I could have hit the boat with a cast, they caught the fish so close. Though I have no evidence for the belief, only the faith of a fisherman, I am certain the fish would have been mine, had the boat pushed on down.

That was strike one for the day's fishing, but I couldn't let one such minor tragedy ruin my day, so I fished down the run and moved on down to the next, directly across the river from the first run I'd wanted, which is a named run called White Creek Run. The named run fishes better than the unnamed one on the back side where I was able to fish, but the run on the back side doesn't get fished much, so I had high hopes. The guy who had reached White Creek Run before I had was still there, and, since conversation was impossible over the roar of the rapid at the run's head, he spread his arms and shrugged his shoulders in the universal sign language for *How you doing?* I shook my head, signifying no action. He raised one finger, signifying a fish or at least a solid take; I decided I should have gotten up earlier.

My side still might hold a fish, so I worked downriver. I was swinging a modestly-sized Royal Blue, a pattern I'd seen in a tying manual and liked the looks of, but had never fished. I made it two-thirds of the way down the run without hooking anything except bottom, though I got my fly back every time it did. Then my rod bucked in my hands as though I'd hooked a horse. I brought up my rod automatically, heart leaping half out of my mouth at the strength of the take, but I hooked nothing, and furthermore I lost my fly. I stripped in line, expecting to find either a straightened hook or a pig's tail of line where my clinch knot had slipped. I found neither. Instead the second knot in the short, aggressively-tapered leader I'd tied to my sink-tip had failed. For the first time in my life, I'd broken off a steelhead on the strike.

Strike two.

I finished out the run, then moved down to a run on the Skagit near the mouth of the Baker. The run below the Baker is better and much longer, but there were already three other anglers thrashing it by the time I arrived, so I backtracked and fished the short run upstream of the Baker. About halfway down I felt yet another thump, but when I raised my rod there was nothing, no sign that I'd had my second strike of the day, the only time I'd had more than one grab in a day and hadn't managed to land a steelhead.

Strike three.

At once, I felt a deep longing grab me, a longing to fish water where I knew one missed strike, one broken off fish, and watching other fishermen catch something were not things to worry over. When I got home I e-mailed my boss in Montana and told him I'd be hitting the road in a few days, as soon as I could arrange storage for all my stuff that wouldn't fit in my Subaru.

•

Yellowstone River, April 25, 2006

On the Yellowstone I got another occasional strike as I worked my way steadily downriver but only picked up two more fish, one brown and another rainbow, both about the same size as the first pair of trout. The patches of river that still had sun shining on them were getting few and far between, now, and I was starting to get discouraged. I was far from despair, but this was not what I had expected when I decided to leave Washington early. The night before I left, an hour before I disconnected my phone and stuffed it in a box with a bunch of other odds and ends, a friend called to give me a report from his recent trip north of the border, where there are more steelhead rivers, many more steelhead, and fewer and more courteous anglers than there are in Washington. He'd landed four, along with a number of large resident cutthroat and bull trout. His partner had hooked a twenty-pound spring Chinook salmon, and the salmon fishing would only get better over the upcoming weeks. I had never made it to British Columbia for steelhead, having dreaded the expensive license and the customs foolishness, and for a moment the prospect grabbed me, though ultimately I left the next morning for Gardiner.

Now, with only four fish landed and two or three missed strikes, and with only spotty fly shop work until late May and few guiding opportunities until sometime in June, I was starting to think that I should have stayed in Bellingham another month. I had experienced the Yellowstone and its tributaries in summer and fall, never spring. Now that I was here, I doubted myself. Based on my lack of success, it seemed the river in spring spoke a language I did not know.

Then I caught another fish. It happened without any particular effort on my part, I just saw my indicator hesitate, I set the hook, and I found myself attached to a fat thirteen-inch rainbow that darted out into the current and jumped twice in quick succession. It got slightly downstream of me, and with the current as its ally, put a moderately impressive bend in my rod. Since I still felt like I was using some sort of fairy wand, for a moment I felt a surge of what can only be described as panic. This fish, like all of the steelhead I have caught, scared me slightly, made me think that I was not in control of the situation. Then the moment passed, I let out the handful of slack I held and got the fish on the reel, and in thirty seconds or so I reached down and netted the pretty male rainbow, bulging from the caddis larva it had been eating when it decided to take my fake one.

I let the fish go without incident and nodded my head. That was more like it. It was also the last fish I caught that day, but that was okay.

The next morning the river was in much better shape. A ten-inch rainbow took on my first cast, and I skidded it home in a moment. Another took on my second cast, but it wriggled free before I could bring it to hand. I might have laughed then, as I tend to do this when I lose average or small fish and know that another will soon follow. After checking my hook to make sure it was sharp, I moved upstream.

Things I Hate About Fly Fishing

I hate it when I'm hiking out after fishing and the game trail I'm following shows why "game" know how to use all four limbs, crumbling under me and sending me tumbling fifty vertical feet through sagebrush and prickly-pear and off an undercut bank into the Gardner River. Especially when the fishing has been slow, leaving me little reason to be happy about being back in the water besides the opportunity to wash out the prickly-pear spines.

Or when the lodgepole trunk I've stepped on dozens of times while walking to or from my secret run on the Yellowstone decides that, this time, it wants to roll under me, sending me falling headfirst downhill. Especially when I fall on a knob where a branch once was, a fire-hardened knob that catches me in the side and makes me think, for several terrifying seconds, that I've cracked a rib or two. *Most* especially when I do this on my birthday.

Or when a herd of bison decides to cross the river where I'm fishing, forcing me to hide between two boulders, hoping they don't see me or hear me and decide to step on my face in case I'm a predator in two-legged disguise. Actually, at the time it's rather amazing, and is only irritating in hindsight, and when the fish is big. Especially when the fish is big (it usually is).

Or when a herd of teenagers comes floating down the river on tubes when I'm guiding clients in the drift boat. They go much more quickly than I do, and usually seem to get in the way when I've got the boat in position to fish a particularly good eddy or current seam, or they dive into a rapid right after I do, forcing me to dodge swimmers as well as Whitebeard waves that could swamp the boat, sending me and my elderly clients into the drink. This always happens when it's hot and sunny and the fishing is terrible, of course, and the kids seem to be having a great deal more fun than my clients and I. It's especially frustrating when my clients are southerners, comfortable in the blazing heat, and don't want me to pull the boat over to take a dip.

Or, when I'm working a good run, I really hate it when a guide comes along with his clients and high banks me, because I'm fishing good water that he wants his big-tipping clients to be able to fish. Especially when *I've* been guiding a lot, and have my first chance for some relaxation in a long time.

Of course, the thing I hate the most, the thing I really can't stand, is when I've been alone for a long time on a certain swift mountain creek with rapids almost tall enough to be called waterfalls, the water's surface turning metallic with the last light of the fading dusk and the noise of the night birds and tumbling stream blending into one, is when I have to go home. Sometimes I stand at my turn-around point until all light is gone, bathed in spray from the plunge that gives the stream its power, a silver curtain over a hundred feet tall, whose waters seem to hold the light the longest, until it reflects only starlight.

Four Scenes: Why and How I Became a Fishing Guide and Why I Still Am

One: Poolside, August 2000

I stared out at the same pool where I'd been a lifeguard for the past five summers, a pool I now managed. In the shallow end, one of the ancient blue-haired witches who thought she owned the place scowled at the twelve-year-old girl drifting by on a raft. The breeze had pushed the girl across the pool into the old lady's path, an affront if ever there was one. The old monster shoved the kid out of her way, waking her up and making her fall off with a splash.

One of my teenage lifeguards was sitting next to me, making bedroom eyes when she wasn't watching the pool. In my idle moments, I made them right back, age difference and immorality of boss-employee relationships be damned. I needed something, anything, to break the monotony of what had been a long, long summer. Besides, she liked to fly fish. I'd been fishing myself all of twice since May, and both times Bennett Spring had been packed solid with morons aiming only to get their five stockers for the frying pan. To add insult to injury, the Pale Evening Duns hadn't revealed themselves, and there had been only one sporadic midge hatch. Not good.

In the deep end, that cop who was always off-duty was between his girlfriend's legs again. He liked to leave his wife at home with the kids when he was taking advantage of the pool's "cops swim free" policy. He came to the pool every day, for hours. I thought about telling them to cut it out, but only for a moment. I had been yelling at him and his skank all summer, and recently a friend had overheard the cop ranting about how he was looking for an excuse to arrest me, so it seemed prudent to lay low for another two weeks. Then I'd head back to school and I'd be free of that horrible job. There was no way I was going to be a lifeguard again. People shouldn't stay at jobs they start on their fifteenth birthday as long as I had.

I was barely 20 and already felt like I was at the end of my rope. It was time for a change.

•

Two: An Apartment Scene, October 2000

After class on Monday, I strapped on my Strat, dimed my amplifier, and proceeded to rock out. After

29

a few minutes, just as I was getting the kinks out, my roommate came home and flopped down on the couch. He turned *on* the TV. He turned *up* the TV. Since the TV was plugged into my stereo system, Jerry Springer got quite loud, loud enough to interfere with my playing.

I snapped off my amp and muttered something that would have gotten bleeped if I were on the show, the only sort of words I'd directed at my roommate in weeks. Normally I'd have gone in my room and played through headphones, but the midterm stress was bad enough only volume or fly fishing had a hope of cracking it. I'd fished the Table Rock tailwater on the White River over the weekend, and the browns and weird fall-spawning stocked rainbows had been running, which helped the stress. Every local knew they were running, which didn't. Elbowing my way into a patch of water amid the snaggers and trophy hunters was something even the 25-inch rainbow I'd caught on a Brassie and 7X couldn't quite make up for. Forty minutes of wholesome family hell while stuck in traffic in Branson on the way back to school was enough to bring back most of the stress.

Even college wasn't enough. Fly fishing in the Midwest wasn't enough. I needed to go back to Yellowstone.

•

Three: In Front of the Computer, February 2001

Though there was some variation, no matter how I ran the spreadsheet program it always came out the same: if I had to live in Yellowstone flipping burgers at minimum wage in one of the hotel restaurants, which was the summer job I'd been offered, there was no way I could so much as break even and still fish at least three days a week.

I worked through the calculations again and again, but with any remotely realistic budget for fly tying materials and flies I would wind up in the red, something I couldn't afford to do if I wanted to stay in school. Damn.

"You've got mail," said the computer. "Fishing in Yellowstone," said the subject line.

I opened the message eagerly, thinking it would be somebody replying to the question I'd posted online earlier in the week. I'd asked about fishing the Firehole River early in the season, which I'd never done. My previous fishing trips to Yellowstone Country had been in July and August, when the Firehole is way too warm to fish well. It wasn't a reply to my question. It was something better.

It read: "My name's Pat Straub, and I used to work for a guy named Richard Parks, owner of Parks' Fly Shop, in Gardiner, Montana, at Yellowstone's North Entrance. From your post, it sounds like you know what you're doing, and he's hiring shop staff and part-time guides for the upcoming season. You should give him a call. It's not a huge shop so you won't be working every day, but you'll have plenty of time to fish. If you work for Richard you'll make way more money and have way more fun than if you work for a Park concessionaire."

Me, a guide? What? I'd only been fly fishing since I was six and tying since I was twelve and had only written a half-dozen magazine articles about either. I'd only been fly fishing in Yellowstone Park since I was thirteen. That couldn't be enough experience, could it?

Of course it could.

Hallelujah.

.

Four: The Yellowstone Drainage, May 2001

The scent of the evergreens was the first thing I noticed when I rolled down the window to pay for my Yellowstone Park entrance permit. Even twenty miles back, in Sunlight Basin, where I'd gotten out of the car to giggle and make snowballs with fistfuls of corn snow from the rotting snowbanks alongside the road, the sweet piney smell had not been so strong. The second thing I noticed was that Soda Butte Creek was not so muddy here as it had been a few miles back. This early in the morning, the day's ration of snowmelt had yet to get this far downstream. I could make out a few rocks that would provide cover, and there were likely-looking pockets all along the undercuts.

The creek grew and grew as I drove downstream into the Park, as the Absaroka Range faded away to east and west. The undercuts got bigger, the pools deeper. Though down here runoff had transformed Round Prairie and Soda Butte Creek's Lower Meadow into vast lakes, I could barely keep my eyes on the road. This was the first time I had laid eyes on Soda Butte Creek, and already I was smitten. The Yellowstone at the bottom of its Grand Canyon, where the Northeast Entrance Road crosses it, affected me similarly. No creek in Missouri possessed the luscious meanders and undercut banks of Soda Butte, and no river I've ever seen can compare to the vast, swift, bouldery Yellowstone.

On the remainder of the drive to Gardiner, I crossed several old friends, rivers and creeks I'd fished as a tourist over the past eight years: Blacktail Creek and Lava, the Gardner River. All were swollen with snowmelt but recognizable. Every stream I saw flowed eventually into the Yellowstone in its canyons, and I wanted to fish every one. Though I didn't know it as I unloaded my gear in the ratty little room I was renting for the summer, I would fish the Yellowstone and its tributaries more than any others over the next fourteen years and counting, would not leave Gardiner or waters in the Yellowstone region except temporarily, to take care of transitory matters like fishing other new and exotic places and finishing my Bachelor's degree at my Midwestern school and a Master's in English in Washington.

More than anything else, the rivers are the blue threads weaving through Yellowstone Park that have bound me to the place. Guys I've worked with and clients I've guided have come and gone, but the rivers have remained.

My First Time

My first time was with Elise. We'd been dating about five months when her parents invited me to spend the weekend with them down on their farm in the Ozarks, where they had acres of old meadows and even older woods where a couple of teenagers could get lost, if they wanted to. They also had three farm ponds, which interested me more than the woods and meadows did, at least when the bluegill were rising. I was 17, she was 15, and neither of us had ever done it, or even gotten very close. Thus, we were both very nervous and very naïve beside Catfish Pond when she took my fly rod in her hands and I took her in my arms, hands covering hers, and slowly began to move with her in the smooth and slow motions required to cast a dry fly with a soft rod.

Over the next forty-five minutes, as the light failed and the swallows were replaced by bats, we caught maybe a dozen bluegill and small bass that were rising to mayflies along the edge of the pond. As we fished I could feel the quiver of the rod through her hands, could feel her quickened heart rate as she learned the smooth motions I was showing her, the way to cast a fly so that the motion becomes something closely akin to art. In this moment, more than many others, we were almost one. Afterwards, when the sun had sunk so far beneath the ridge to the west that we could no longer see even the enormous Renegade I had tied on, we lay down side by side in the grass beside the pond to look at the stars, and the *clop* sounds of bluegill rising to duns punctuated our conversation as we talked about life and love and fishing. She was eager to do it again. Sometimes I still regret that we never did.

But I've sure enjoyed fishing with other girls.

Lamar River Blues

The best day of fishing I've ever had on the Lamar River was the 4th of July, 2001. I spent four hours in the upper end of the river's second canyon, the one right next to the road, working my way upstream around the house-sized boulders and climbing the edges of the 45-degree cascades that the kayakers supposedly hunger after. The Salmonflies were out in force, and the fish wanted them. Moreover, this section of the Lamar is so steep that I didn't have to worry about sharing a single foot of it with anyone else. I was in heaven.

I started off just upstream of the Slough Creek Campground Road, descending into the canyon down a steep sage-covered slope and at last by a slide down a giant flood-smoothed boulder, and finished at the very top of the canyon, where the road comes down to meet the river. Along the way, I caught maybe fifty fish. Or it might have been sixty, or forty-five.

Honestly I have no idea. A few minutes after I started I realized I was going to catch enough fish that even trying to keep count wasn't necessary.

Every single fish I caught ate an adult Salmonfly pattern. I started with the venerable Parks' Salmonfly, the first "improved" Sofa Pillow pattern and one that has proven its worth for Parks' Fly Shop guides and customers since 1954. I only had two of them, and I soon lost the first to an errant backcast and the other to the destructive potential of large cutthroat trout. Then I proceeded to go through all my Matt's Stones and all but one of my largest Yellowstone X patterns, about eight flies in all. I fished each fly until I lost it or until it was completely destroyed, and I rose many, many trout to every one of them.

And a lot of the trout were big. Most were between ten and fourteen inches, about average for this stretch of the Lamar, but there were at least six between seventeen and nineteen inches. Of these, two came on bow-and-arrow casts into small eddies between the bank and the steepest cascade on the entire river, a hundred yard stretch of river that drops fifty feet, pinched between banks so steep that at times I had to toss my rod uphill ahead of me and use both hands to climb to the next casting position. I love this kind of water because I usually have it to myself, and though there are fewer fish in it than flatter stretches, due to less adequate holding water, they don't see the pressure their cousins do and thus rise eagerly, especially during the Salmonfly hatch.

I couldn't see much of the scenery because the Lamar canyon is narrow and has tall lodgepole pines on both banks, uphill of the boulder fields that line the river's course, but the narrow slot of sky between the trees was that gorgeous deep blue that I've only seen in the high country, and the wind was fitful but not blowing hard enough to make casting a chore, even though the Lamar Canyon can funnel the typical afternoon gusts out of the southwest into a gale. It was even a nice temperature, about 70 degrees, warm enough to make wet-wading comfortable but not hot enough to bring out too much sweat when I had to work hard to make my way upstream (and uphill) through the boulder fields.

In other words, this was a day of fishing worth remembering, and more than that, worth remembering well enough to write about. Perhaps best of all, I had the next day off too, and I planned to return with plenty more fake Salmonflies. The weather report claimed conditions on the 5th would be about the same, and the only thing a single day would do to change things would be to reduce the number of Salmonflies in the air somewhat, since the peak of the hatch was just passing. This would make the fish pay still more attention to my flies, since they'd have less competition from real bugs. I had no reason to believe fishing wouldn't be just as good.

The next day, the weather was the same, the water conditions were the same, and there were about 3/4 as many Salmonflies in the air. Fishing conditions were optimal. I was on the stretch of the canyon immediately downstream of where I'd started the day before, a difference of only a mile or so, not enough to matter, and saw no sign any other anglers had beat me to the river that morning. In fact, it looked like the water I was on hadn't been fished for days.

I caught two fish in an hour, the largest nine inches long. This was my first experience of the

Lamar's typical weirdness, which I call the Lamar River Blues.

•

In a region famed for good trout fishing, the Lamar stands out. It's not any better than its tributaries or the Yellowstone into which it feeds. It's notable both because it's good and because its fish are the least predictable of any in the area. Trout in Slough Creek are usually more finicky, and mostly bigger, while those in Soda Butte trend slightly smaller and are slightly easier to catch. Even though the fish are harder to catch on Slough, they are *consistently* hard to catch. You might run into a dense hatch that brings most every fish to the surface, but even if you do the well-educated trout in that stream are just as likely to turn away from your best presentation as to bite. On the Lamar, the fish might rise to the same hatch with such abandon that you could probably throw a Royal Wulff three sizes too large over their heads, skate it back, and catch all the fish you could want. At other times, a riffle corner might boil with emerging Green Drakes or PMDs, but lack a single rising fish.

The usual explanation for this behavior on the part of the Lamar's fish is that they move a lot more than stream-dwelling trout tend to do. While some radio-tagged fish that live near the confluence with Soda Butte Creek have been found to move in and out of this tributary regularly, an alternate explanation for this is that the Lamar upstream from Soda Butte can get quite warm in late summer, while Soda Butte stays cold. For fish above Soda Butte, moving downstream and then up into the creek makes sense. For those below, in water now cooled by the addition of the large tributary (Soda Butte usually carries almost as much water as the Lamar itself where the two streams meet, by the beginning of August), this migration is unnecessary.

At any rate, my first experience of the Lamar River Blues took place in the river's canyon, where the river's steep gradient makes day-to-day migrations by the trout of more than a few yards impossible. I have a different answer for why the trout in the canyon didn't respond on the 5th, and why those in the upper river can be so frustrating: because sometimes they feel like being annoying.

This is an anthropocentric idea, of course, but fishing is an anthropocentric sport to begin with, though it can lead to a non-anthropocentric appreciation of the natural world. We go out to a river and take pride in the fact that we fool an animal with "a brain the size of a pea," as the saying goes, into eating the fake food we provide. Though sometimes the environment in which the sport takes place or the epiphanies that can come upon us when we fish become more important than the fish themselves, it's important to remember that sport fishing is something we do for fun, an activity in which the fish join unwillingly. When we say "the fish were aggressive today" or "I fooled that one!" we are assigning human motivations to the fish. It should work both ways. Instead of blaming the weather or environmentally-dictated migrations when the fish don't cooperate, we should give the fish the agency to say "I don't feel like it today," and blow a raspberry at us.

Or at least that's an interesting way of looking at the whole situation, one that makes it less frustrating when we run into situations like the one I did on the 5th of July. Rather than wondering what the fish are thinking or what their motivations are when they do something we can't explain, the real question might be why we put up with it.

It's been said many times that people would not fish if it were always good. It would get boring. This is probably true for most of us. I know it is for me. Yet there's a difference between a certain measure of unpredictability and what the Lamar can offer. On the 4th, I hadn't known what to expect at all. I hadn't fished the river since the 21st of June, when it was still high, cold, and dirty and I had to fish nymphs and streamers to get any action, so it was a pleasant surprise that the Salmonflies were out. This was unpredictability, which has been reduced now that I am a lot more experienced at fishing in Yellowstone Park and know the Lamar usually has adult Salmonflies in sufficient numbers for the fish to eat them about a week after they on the Yellowstone downstream of Gardiner. Going from the best day of fishing I've ever had on a river to the worst, when nothing besides the date seemed to have changed, goes beyond mere unpredictability.

That might be the answer. We like unpredictability, yet everything we do as fishermen besides going to new rivers minimizes this unpredictability, keeps it within certain boundaries. I make my living off of this fact. Most of the anglers I guide have at least some idea what they're doing, and many aren't all that interested in the casting and aquatic entomology lessons I have to offer. What they want help with is fly selection and picking a spot to fish in a region that has literally hundreds of worthwhile streams and tens of thousands of good spots on these streams. Most expect to catch more fish with me than without, but they expect what I tell them to carry over to their own fishing later. Instead of going from (hopefully) a lot of trout to none or a handful, they might catch more than they've ever caught before on their guided trip, followed by a day fishing on their own when they don't catch as many as they did on the guided day, but more than they would have caught if they had just gone up to the river blind.

To be able to meet great success one day and fair success the next, consistently, doesn't seem like much uncertainty to me.

The occasional skunking is to be expected, and the usual reply when someone retells the sad tale of such a day, or a trip when two fish are caught following one where the angler got fifty, is "That's fishing!" Yet if most days resulted in skunkings, or the trout always responded without rhyme or reason, it would cease to be "fishing" and would become "stupid." If there was no way to keep the variation between days to a minimum, what would be the point of honing our skills? Wouldn't luck be the prime factor?

For those who don't see any problem with fish that seemingly operate at random, I recommend taking up fishing for winter-run steelhead.

•

If most fishermen try to minimize the unpredictability of their trips, or at least aim to keep unpredictability within narrowly-defined limits, it would seem reasonable for the Lamar to go unfished. When there's a hatch on Soda Butte, a skilled angler will catch lots of fish if he or she has the right flies, period. When there's a hatch on Slough Creek, a skilled angler will probably catch fewer fish and have to work harder for them, but there's a good chance a couple of these trout will crack twenty inches. When there's a good hatch on the Lamar, nobody knows what might happen.

Fly anglers are a squirrelly bunch, so maybe I'm wrong about the Lamar's unpredictability being a turn-off. Some people do hate to fish the river, yet it gets more press than most rivers in Yellowstone and virtually every access point save those in the canyon has a car or two in it when the river is fishable, so it's certainly not suffering from a lack of anglers.

Still, there's another explanation to this fact besides that fly anglers are masochists: the other rivers and streams in the area. The Lamar has two world-class tributaries in Slough Creek and Soda Butte, several of its backcountry tributaries offer fast fishing for smaller trout than those in the Lamar itself, and the Yellowstone a few miles away is even more famous than the Lamar. With all these options, there are plenty of places nearby where it is fairly easy to predict what the trout will be doing on a given day. If the trout aren't biting on the Lamar despite all evidence that they should, odds are that they'll be eating hoppers on the Yellowstone or Flavs on Soda Butte. If all else fails, the brook trout in upper Tower, Blacktail, and many other small creeks are almost always hungry, and there might be a big brown or two in the Gardner or the Madison.

Such is Yellowstone Park. While the Lamar might leave a bitter taste in one's mouth after its fish pull a disappearing act for no apparent reason, there are plenty of other places that will offer a sweeter taste. None of Yellowstone Park's rivers are the "best" rivers of a given character in the country, probably, but nowhere else is such a variety of water available within a small geographic area. Good meals almost always feature a variety of flavors, and fishing works the same way. Maybe the Lamar wouldn't get fished as often as it does if it were a destination river far from other worthwhile fisheries, but since it is so close to so much water that can produce almost as well when the fishing is good and remain more consistent even when it's bad, many anglers are willing to get the Lamar River Blues, on the off chance that instead of tough fishing they'll have a day like I did on the 4th of July, 2001. With so much other water nearby it's unlikely that their blues will continue for more than a day, or however long it takes them to give up and go somewhere else. When it is not considered alone, the Lamar's inherent strangeness ceases to be a concern. While it might be unpredictable, the streams around it are not, which serves to make the entire area consistent, with just enough uncertainty so that it never gets boring.

A remaining possibility is that all of these explanations and justifications might just be another way of blaming something other than poor fishing skills or the inherent weirdness of trying to catch trout on little bits of feather and fur lashed to a hook rather than in a net or with dynamite for failure, and that's fine. Trout fishing is not politics or business, so it's not morally reprehensible to shrug off responsibility for failure in the sport once in a while, though the flipside is that we shouldn't always credit our fishing skills on days when we do well. That's easier said than done, especially on a river like the Lamar, where everything seems so out of control.

After all, there's always a chance that it wasn't my fault or the fault of the fish that made the fifth such a poor day, but a reminder from the Trout Gods that it isn't always supposed to be good, especially on a river I knew had a reputation for weirdness. And that's fine too. On a river where fish vanish from day to day and dense hatches might go ignored, in the fairy-tale setting of Yellowstone, belief in Trout Gods makes a lot more sense than it usually does. It also makes it less painful to throw up one's hands and go fish the Yellowstone or Soda Butte when the fishing is bad, rather than grimly sticking it out as if the Lamar were the only good river in the area. If the gods will it, who's to argue?

Tangible Evidence of
Trout Gods

I had something of a crisis of faith when I was thirteen. For a year or two I'd modified my Catholic faith with a caveat based on my years as a Boy Scout and appreciation of both the natural world and my skewed understanding of Native American religion. I decided arbitrarily that God had two sons, Jesus and The Great Spirit, with Jesus doing the work in the Old World and The Great Spirit taking care of things in the New. From the start I knew it didn't make much sense to tell anyone else about this new religion, which probably saved me some ridicule.

By my thirteenth birthday, I realized my new religion was complete bullshit. This left me with something of a void, however. It should be obvious that Catholicism wasn't cutting it for me, yet I was not ready to give up on religion completely. With

Confirmation coming in the fall, I was left wondering if I should actually go through with it. I decided to do so, not least because of the presents I could expect. I'd received my first fly vest as a gift after my First Communion, the last big sacrament I'd had, and I really needed a new pair of waders.

My thirteenth summer was a difficult time in my fly fishing career, as well. I'd been reading M. R. Montgomery, John Gierach, and Robert Traver for a year or so, since a well-meaning relative had purchased a lot of used fly fishing books for me at an auction. I don't think my aunt realized these books would push my involvement in the sport from a pastime to an addiction. When I started reading, I was primed to enter stage three of my fly fishing career.

Stage one lasted from age six or seven until ten or eleven, and involved the fewest fish. I grew up fishing streams in the Missouri Ozarks that are stocked daily, so in the morning I'd fling spinners and catch three or four, then switch to my fly rod and catch nothing for the rest of the day, but would happily watch my giant strike indicator for any indication the micro-jig or egg fly underneath had interested a trout. I could do this all day long and not complain, and when I did actually catch a fish, it was a major victory.

At some point I transitioned seamlessly into stage two, during which I grew adept at interesting the stockers on the odd things Missouri anglers call flies: enormous egg patterns, jigs, "fur bugs," and small flesh flies designed to imitate the entrails of less-fortunate stockers caught early in the day, which the few quasi-holdover fish quickly learn are a great source of protein. It was disgusting fishing, though I didn't realize it at the time. I caught a lot of fish, but it wasn't pretty.

Stage three began March 6, 1993, when I was almost thirteen. Gierach and company had me well-primed for a change, and a stupendous Blue-winged Olive hatch pushed me over the edge. It was early enough in the season that most of the fish in that Ozark spring creek were true holdovers who had survived the winter on real food. They fought better, rose better, and lived in more interesting stretches of stream than the dredged pools where the stockers were dumped. And fishing for them with dry flies made me feel like a real fly fisherman.

The flesh flies and jigs were put away soon after in favor of dries. Many of these were Western patterns totally unsuited to Midwestern spring creeks, but they were patterns favored by the writers, so I had to try them. While it was obvious from both my reading and the film version of *A River Runs through It* that real fly fishermen used dries, it was also obvious that sometimes one had to tie on a nymph. Therefore, considering myself a sophisticated fly fisherman, I'd deign to fish nymphs as well as dries. There were two problems with this sudden transition: I had almost no idea how to catch trout holding in proper lies and eating proper foods, and I was used to catching enough bewildered stockers that going fishless while learning to catch holdovers was a painful experience.

Thus on the eve of my first trip to Montana, in July of 1993, the usual crises of a thirteen-year-old boy, namely pimples and impressing the two girls in school with breasts larger than mosquito bites, were joined in my case with uncertainty in my religious identity and in my fly fishing identity. The latter

48

problem would not be fully solved until years later, when I entered stage five of my development as a fly angler, the phase in which I moved to Montana and became a guide, but my religious issues would be resolved in a moment as I stood out of breath after charging down a narrow spring creek after a runaway trout.

•

Bennett Spring Branch, the stream I fished most of the time, appears in many of the magazines and even national newspapers on a semi-regular basis, though not for good reasons. On March 1, Opening Day, something on the order of three thousand people show up to crowd a mile and a half of spring creek to fling flies, spinners, and various neon-colored baits at five thousand trout stocked the night before and perhaps a thousand that made it through the previous season and survived the winter. It is almost always crowded through the summer, as well, with somewhere between three hundred and a thousand people commonly present throughout the March 1-October 31 catch & keep season (the winter catch & release season is far more enjoyable. Needless to say, in stage three I had a hard time finding places to fish, since standing almost shoulder-to-shoulder at the edge of one of the dredged pools where the stocking truck dumps trout every night is not an ideal place to daintily cast an Adams.

My favorite place was the hatchery outlet, a hundred yards of artificial creek a rod-length wide overhung by trees and lined by grass and fly-eating bushes. When I return to Missouri during Bennett Spring's catch & release season, I still enjoy fishing it. Perhaps realizing it didn't make any sense to dredge and otherwise disfigure this short stretch of stream as they had the rest of the creek, so as to fit those 3,000 anglers, the state DNR left this stretch alone. Only in Missouri could an artificial stream seem more natural than the natural stream into which it runs.

Since it seems natural, with gravel allowed to come to rest where the spring and fall floods place it and aquatic plants left to grow instead of trimmed back to present less of a threat to the spinner-tossing hordes, it is a good place to cast flies imitating natural foods for trout that have learned to survive on insects and smaller fish rather than Purina Trout Chow. I knew this even at thirteen, even if I did not fully know how to fish the appropriate flies or how to approach the water and conduct myself while fishing what is, in essence, a miniature gin-clear spring creek that is nowhere more than waist-deep and seldom even comes to the knees of a thirteen-year-old who hasn't hit his growth spurt yet.

As a case in point, picture me charging down the middle of the creek as fast as I could go, my rod pointed straight out ahead of me to slip beneath the screen of overhanging branches. I was walking in the middle of the creek because this was the only place where the branches and bushes made travel easy, and I was going quickly because this was the only way I knew at the time to walk in a creek without having the mud plume I created by shuffling my feet overtake me, thereby making it impossible for me to spot fish downstream. Though I often fished dry flies in the hatchery outlet, I almost always used to work downstream, for the simple but not satisfactory reason that it was a shorter walk to the upstream end of the outlet than to its mouth.

The previous paragraph should make it clear why I didn't catch many fish in those days. I seldom even saw any that weren't dashing away in terror, save for recent stockers who thought humans meant lunchtime, which were, since I was in stage three and starry-eyed from reading Gierach and so on, undesirable.

But for whatever reason, on this day in July I did see a holdover fish before I spooked it. I froze at once, the mud plume overran me, and the fish disappeared into the cloud of muck. Despite the mud I kept still, and perhaps I held my breath. For two minutes the cloud of mud washed on down the creek, then began to thin. The fish was still there. It was spooked, clearly, as it was lying on the bottom almost motionless, not feeding. Yet it was still there, and as I watched it began to feed again, darting back and forth in the now-clear current to grab nymphs.

The fish was holding in a narrow micro-riffle with a gravel bottom below a wider stretch with weed beds along both banks, an ideal feeding location. The fish was not particularly large in the grand scheme of things, sixteen inches or so, but most Missouri stockers are ten to twelve inches long, with some going fourteen inches. Though once in a while someone catches a five- or six-pounder that makes its living eating guts, sculpins, and stockers, and the stream record is actually a sixteen-pound leviathan brown trout, the sixteen-incher was still a very, very good fish for Bennett Spring.

I wanted it.

As usual, I'd been fishing an Adams, purely out of optimism since nothing was hatching and Bennett Spring trout usually don't rise unless there's a hatch.

By the fish's feeding behavior, I knew that I needed to tie on a nymph. I clipped off the Adams and discovered that I needed a new tippet. I pulled out my sole spool of tippet, 5X, and discovered I only had three inches left. I also only had a dollar and some change in my pocket, which meant I couldn't walk over to the park store to buy a new spool. With maybe five inches of tippet left on the end of my leader, I'd get one shot. If the fish didn't like the fly I chose, there'd be nothing for me to do but walk a mile back upstream to where my dad was fishing and beg a few bucks to buy myself some more tippet. It was too late in the afternoon to make this walk, turn around and walk down to the store to buy a new spool, and get back to the hatchery outlet before the end of legal fishing hours.

So I chose carefully, selecting my favorite nymph at the time, a pale-bodied #16 Gold-ribbed Hare's Ear. I almost never fish Hare's Ears anymore, but at the time it was one of only two or three nymphs I carried. It may not have made sense to have great faith in a fly that seldom produced more than the zero trout I usually caught, regardless of what I was fishing, but I did. If I was going to catch the trout, it was going to be on the Hare's Ear.

There was one further wrinkle: I had faith in the Hare's Ear in the hatchery outlet, but none at all anywhere between the hatchery outlet and the pool my dad was fishing. Not only would I only get one shot at the trout ten feet from me that was now darting back and forth with its mouth flashing white every ten or fifteen seconds as it picked off a nymph, this would be my only shot period. Even in these days of not many fish, the single trout I was looking at carried a great deal more meaning than most of the fish I tried to catch.

After I had the fly on, after I'd held it in the water to soak it so it would sink before it reached the trout, there was nothing to do but make my cast. Or perhaps there was one thing.

My heart was pounding by this time. The trout was probably bigger than any other I was likely to catch this trip, and it was certainly a holdover, the sort of trout I wanted to catch. So I offered up a prayer. I didn't offer this prayer to any of the deities I prayed to in those days, definitely not to the Great Spirit, Jesus, or God, and I didn't say "amen" at the end. There's only one group of supernatural beings that possibly fit as recipients: the Trout Gods. Seek and ye shall find. Here's the prayer: "If you let me catch this fish, I'll let it go."

Nowadays I release most of the fish I catch. This season I've kept three, all brookies from a mountain pond. When I was thirteen, things were different. I didn't keep everything I caught, since a few six-inch stockers always make it into the stream before they're grown up enough to be there, but I was always smiles when I caught my limit of five fish big enough to fit in the pan. It didn't happen very often, I can assure you. Since holdover trout taste much better than recent stockers, offering to let the trout go was doubly a sacrifice. I figured offering such a sacrifice to the Trout Gods would get me the fish.

The Trout Gods must have been pleased, because on the first drift the fish turned slightly to its right, pinwheeled its pectoral fins to tilt upwards a fraction, and inhaled my Hare's Ear with a flash of its white mouth. It ate with total confidence, just like my fly was any other nymph. Despite the massive and usually catastrophic deficiencies in my fly fishing skills, I was actually quite used to sight-nymphing, since stockers learn to spit fake food as quickly as they grab it, what with so many kids tossing bits of gravel into the hatchery rearing channels to giggle at the fruitless feeding frenzies they cause. So I didn't set the hook too hard or too soon, and was rewarded immediately with a headshake. Then all hell broke loose.

I was standing upstream of the fish, so it had nowhere to go but down. It clearly did not appreciate being hooked, and thought the best way to show this dissatisfaction was to run screaming the other way. Seldom have I had a trout run more than a few feet in the narrow confines of the hatchery outlet, especially in the smaller and slower upper portion where I was fishing. This trout not only ran out the slack I held in my hand but started peeling line off my reel, as well. It never got more than twenty feet from me, but I followed it fifty feet downstream to keep things so close.

Besides this one amazing run, the fight was not flashy, nor particularly long. Trout, like painters, are more likely to display flash and panache when given a large canvas, and the hatchery outlet is anything but. For one thing, it's so shallow that the trout couldn't gain enough leverage to jump, but instead thrashed wildly on the surface. The difficult part was threading my rod through the screens of brush and overhanging branches while still keeping enough pressure on the trout that it didn't get off. As the fish ran downstream, I worried that if it reached the plunge pool where the second hatchery outlet spills over an artificial waterfall to join the main outlet I was fishing, it would be gone. The opposite turned out to be true. While the fish ran into the spray below the plunge, instead of using the force of the increased current to continue on downstream towards the main channel of the spring branch, it took refuge in the plunge pool itself. This allowed me to retrieve a great deal of line, so that in a minute or two I was standing where the bottom just starts to drop off into the dark green depths of the plunge pool. I could see the fish sitting down on the bottom, worn out. Unless something fluky happened, the fish would be mine.

When I realized this, I decided to keep the trout, despite my promise. Perhaps unreasonable with a shot of fresh adrenaline in my system, I thought my dad either wouldn't believe I had landed such a large trout in the first place or would be angry that I let it go instead of popping it on the head for dinner. Remember that I was thirteen, and therefore not prone to rational decisions.

Thus I was consciously planning on reneging on my promise as I brought my rod tip back to bring the fish to my net. With the rod not quite vertical enough to get the net under the trout, the rod tip caught on an unseen branch over my head. Concentrating on the trout, I jerked my wrist back and forth to free the rod, rather than looking up to see what it was caught on. This usually works. It didn't this time, so I jerked harder. This time the tip came loose, but it didn't sound quite right. I didn't pay much attention at the time, because now I had the trout in my net and was too busy admiring it to pay attention to anything else. Recently-stocked hatchery trout are washed-out watercolors, with silvery-gray sides and a pale pink strip, with backs of darker gray with perhaps a bare touch of green. The trout I held in my net was an oil painting. Its belly was still white, but its sides were more gold than silvery-gray, its stripe was at least an inch wide and crimson, and its back was olive green.

As I was unhooking the fish, something slid down my line and bumped against my arm. After getting the fish situated in the bottom of my net, where it'd be easier to get it on my stringer without it flopping back into the creek, I looked down at whatever bumped me. It was the first three inches of my rod tip.

I'd broken windows, lied to my parents, egged my teacher's house, and done everything else thirteen-year-old boys are supposed to feel guilty about. Sometimes I'd felt guilty. Usually I didn't. I'd never felt more guilty than I did when I saw that rod tip. Apparently my line had gotten wrapped around both rod and branch, so by jerking at it I was jerking the last bit of tip against a pivot point only three inches down rather than allowing the entire rod to flex. An encounter with a car door would have been no more effective in breaking the rod. The worst part was that I knew I deserved it. I'd made a promise five minutes before and broken it without much thought. My faith in the Christian God was on the downswing, but standing there holding my broken rod I it was now crystal clear that there were gods who controlled rivers and whether or not the trout would bite. I had just pissed them off royally and now I was suffering for it.

I'd like to say I released the trout at that moment, but I figured I had my punishment, so I didn't let it go. Walking in heavy bootfoot waders is a slow process anywhere at any time, but it's especially slow in July in Missouri when it's 90 degrees out and the air feels like a wool blanket, and you have to stop every fifty feet to dip your trout in the water to for a few breaths to keep it from dying prematurely and starting to rot. This meant I had plenty of time to castigate myself and worry as I made my way upstream to my dad. Like most thirteen-year-olds I had no money, and I was two weeks out from the most exciting trip a young Gierach fan could reasonably expect to take, my first trip to the hallowed waters of Yellowstone and Montana. I didn't have any hope of making enough money to replace my (one) fly rod prior to the trip. Various visions filled my head: I wouldn't be able to fish at all. I'd have to use my *spinning rod.*

My dad was impressed by the fish, which as I'd expected was a good two inches longer than anything he'd caught. He was more impressed by my stricken expression. I showed him the rod tip, expecting it to explain everything. I was amazed when he shrugged. "It's not a big deal," he said. "We'll take it to Charlie in the morning and he'll fix it. Rods get broken."

"But it will cost too much! The break is too far down just to put a new tip guide on."

"It's a clean break, he can match the ends and reattach them with graphite. Haven't you ever looked closely at Grandpa's rod?"

I hadn't. After my dad gave me the keys to the truck and took charge of my fish, I went to get the rod my dad had inherited from my grandpa. Two inches further down the rod than where I'd broken mine there was a smooth football-shaped swelling where a break had been repaired seamlessly. I put my busted rod in the truck and removed Grandpa's, jointed it, and gave it a wiggle. It felt fine. I later learned that my grandpa'd fished that rod for ten years without a problem, after breaking it. We took my rod to Charlie Reading's shop in the morning and in forty-five minutes it was almost as good as new. My dad loaned me the thirty bucks the repair cost.

I knew at the time and still know I was granted a reprieve. The Trout Gods don't require much in the way of worship or tithes—a few bucks to Trout Unlimited and some sweat while doing habitat protection work are all they require. Beware if you break deals with them, however. $30 to fix a broken rod tip is nothing. I knew that if I defied them again, the Trout Gods would demand torn waders, a tumble down a cliff into the river or even—perish the thought—a blood sacrifice.

A few years later I finally abandoned the Catholicism I'd insulted by arbitrarily adding a fourth figure to the Holy Trinity, but in the interim I added yet more gods to the pantheon. I didn't know how many, but certainly more than one, since rivers and streams have such different characters. Like the Greeks, I suspect that each stream may have its own particular small god, though unfortunately I've yet to actually see any sexy nymphs while I wander the riverbanks. Though I always felt a bit foolish about my belief in the Great Spirit, I've never felt this way about muttering prayers to the Trout Gods. After all, I've experienced a revelation from them.

Yet there's still one nagging thought that won't go away. Maybe when I'm muttering prayers to the Trout Gods, perhaps I'm actually just praying to the trout. If so, they seem to be listening, often enough.

The Brave Cutthroat

There is no monopoly on courage. It is the quality of courage found in fish that leads men to fish for them.
    ~Steve Raymond, from "The Quality of Courage"

For years, I thought that cutthroats never managed to ascend the stream I'll call Trout Creek past a certain point. Above this point, a narrow chute in which the stream's entire flow is compressed to flow with the force of a fire hydrant for ten horizontal feet and fifteen vertical, I had before caught only brook trout, the fish that dominate upstream of this barrier. Still, I hoped always to find a cutthroat, believing that one must somehow be able to ascend this stretch of whitewater, like a salmon or a steelhead.

Still, though I *hoped*, I never *expected* to actually find a cutt. I had usually managed at least one brook trout when visiting the pockets above the chute, and sometimes several, but I had never so much as hooked a trout whose weight suggested it was a cutthroat.

Then, of course, I caught one. I do not recall the fly I used, though it was probably a dropper nymph hanging under a big hopper. I do remember the pool: the fish was resting comfortably in a pocket behind a boulder in the second pool up from the chute. I could tell immediately upon setting the hook that the trout was no brook trout, or at least that it was a brookie far larger than any I had previously hooked in the creek. Soon, however, I knew the trout was a cutthroat. I was fishing at dusk, but even with the gathering darkness I could see the swirling silver spray as the trout wallowed on the surface. Brook trout bulldog on the bottom, or, if they are small, fly across or over the water towards the angler. Yellowstone cutthroats often wallow on the surface, beginning a fight as though already exhausted, or as though they are drunk. They do not provide the wild battle of a rainbow or the dogged fight of a brown, or at least such is their reputation. For this they are often maligned. Even locals occasionally decry the fish, declaring in bars and fly shops that Yellowstone Park would be better off if every river in it were doused with rotenone and all its rivers stocked with more-storied fish.

I do not feel this way. On an Internet forum, my handle is "Longs for Cutts." Yet I do acknowledge that the allure of Yellowstone cutthroat trout does not come from the battles they provide, but from their surroundings, from their rarity, from the solitude I most often find when pursuing them.

Yet the trout's fight was the furthest thing from my mind as I brought the cutthroat in upper Trout Creek to hand. It was a female stretching fourteen inches, approximately average for the trout that fill the stream from mid-June until mid-August, when they come up to spawn and then hang around to feed in the cold, fertile creek, and though it was healthy it was quite slim. It had simply struggled mightily to climb as far as it had, with the most strenuous challenge also the last. Though I do not clamber around the rocks lining Trout Creek for fun, I once climbed the steep sections of similar rivers in the Missouri Ozarks. On occasion young women, many of them lovely creatures clad in minimalist bikinis to better sun themselves, would call out from their high, rounded boulders that I was brave or fearless. At fifteen or sixteen myself, this was the result I hoped for.

I appreciated being called brave then, but my clambering among the boulders and small chutes and cascades was far less brave than the actions of the cutthroat I held cradled in my hands as I whooped with joy at the opportunity to catch it.

•

Cutthroats have always been Yellowstone's trout, having arrived in the area near the close of the last ice age, when a glacial dam created a relatively low-elevation lake that drained both to the Pacific and the Atlantic. The fish that would become Yellowstone cutts, then indistinguishable from their Snake River finespotted cousins that still inhabit the Snake River drainage to the south and west, literally found a Northwest Passage long before any brave European explorer could do so. A handful still do: far above

Yellowstone Lake, in the mountains that birth the Yellowstone River, Two Ocean Creek runs through a swampy meadow high atop a plateau. At the end of this meadow, the creek splits in two. Pacific Creek is a renowned tributary of the Snake, Atlantic Creek is a renowned tributary of the headwaters of the Yellowstone, entering the river far back in the trackless Thorofare region south of Yellowstone National Park, where grizzlies outnumber humans by a vast margin. Trout at times swim over the top of this divide, creating a limited but noteworthy genetic interchange between populations that are now otherwise unconnected.

Genetic interplay of a different sort occurs downstream of Upper and Lower Falls. Rainbows stocked by misguided fisheries managers starting in the late 1800s have slowly but steadily eroded the Yellowstone Cutthroat's genetic purity by interbreeding with them. In the Grand Canyon of the Yellowstone, one seldom encounters a pure rainbow or cutt-bow, but it does happen on occasion. In the Black Canyon and downstream, past the Yellowstone boundary and on into southern Montana, cutt-bows are far more common. Indeed, it is difficult to gauge at times whether a fish is a pure cutthroat or not. Who knows what species its great-grandparents were?

Despite this interbreeding, strong populations of Yellowstone cutts remain in the Yellowstone River drainage, including most of its tributaries upstream as far as the first large waterfalls, waterfalls they could not ascend. Through most of their range the subspecies has been extirpated, but here, in the highest, coldest, most physically-demanding part of their range, they remain common, and are friends to anglers, especially those who prefer to fish dry flies: Yellowstone cutts are renowned for their willingness to rise.

•

They seldom rise on Trout Lake. Only when the summer Traveling Sedges, the *Callibaetis*, and the occasional damselfly hatches occur do they come up. Yet they do ascend, not to eat but to spawn. They climb the lake's swift, narrow little inlet, a stream that drops out of the hills upstream in a series of stairstep plunges separated by momentary patches of well-aerated gravel suitable for spawning. This little creek is narrow enough to step across, and is nowhere more than eighteen inches deep. Some of its pockets, holding water in miniature, are so small that the cutthroats that ascend the creek brush their heads against the rocks upstream while their tails extend over the plunge below, exposed to air and sun and the watchful eyes of the predators that seek them.

These predators are legion. Bears fish the inlet on occasion, and birds take eggs and fry. A few years ago an ever-resourceful coyote was seen plunging after cutthroats, successfully, and where the inlet stream spreads out into a great, slow fan of ankle-deep water over sand and muck as it enters the lake, a family of otters is often in evidence, taking more trout than the anglers that fish as close to the inlet as they're legally allowed to, or sometimes even closer. There are even some disgusting wastes of flesh who fish the creek itself, flaunting the regulations, poaching this precious resource. I assume many come under cover of night, appropriate for thieves.

Yet despite their many predators, Trout Lake's cutthroats are among the spookiest in Yellowstone, choosing their own food with care even as many of those that seek them do so wantonly, anglers included. Likewise, though they rub their bellies raw and batter themselves in their attempts to ascend their spawning stream, they are large, heavy-bodied and far stronger than most anglers give them credit for before tying into one.

•

The trout in a nameless trickle I know about are not quite so large as those in Trout Lake, but they are not small, either. Most run fourteen inches or so. Yet these trout make an even more impressive climb than the Trout Lake fish.

Their spawning tributary is almost dry in fall, and in spring it roars with high-country snowmelt where it cascades in white froth down a hillside and into the river. Early in the summer and on into early July, it flows just enough to provide spawning gravel for the three or four dozen cutthroats that climb it sixty or seventy vertical feet, or perhaps more. I have followed the creek only a hundred yards or so from its confluence with the Yellowstone, scrambling with difficulty up and around the deadfalls and rocks that choke the almost-ephemeral creek, until the creek comes level with the trail out, and I have seen spawners over this entire distance. Perhaps they continue still further: I had thought two of the barriers downstream (an ugly deadfall jam and a three-foot vertical plunge) would mean the end of the cutthroats, until I surmounted these barriers with great effort myself and saw between three and five fish hovering in the micro-pools above.

I carried my rod when I followed the creek up from the river, but I did not try to fish. Even had I wanted to target spawners, a better method would have been to come softly up behind them and snare them with my hands. Nowhere is this stream more than three feet wide, and in places it is condensed into a hydrant-like six-inch flow. It was above one such stretch where I turned, and standing on tiptoe, could see the top of my car over the rim of the little canyon down which the creek flowed. I was looking slightly downhill at my car, which stood at the edge of a steep descent to the river, down which I do not take some of my clients for fear that they could not climb out again. The cutthroats, all weighing no more than a pound or two and with a far more difficult "trail" to ascend, had climbed a slope that would daunt many people.

·

The Salmonfly hatch is a key moment in the lives of many Westerners, myself included. Even random people in the bar remember how the hatch a while ago got blown out by a 4th of July hailstorm, and actually enjoy talking about it. It's the biggest event of the year for Yellowstone River trout, as well. The cutthroats are right on the bank this time of year, in a few inches of water, because that's where they're more likely to be able to pick off nymphs on their way to shore and adult Salmonflies that fall from the bankside bushes, which are still mostly awash in the fading runoff. The trout feed voraciously, apparently without fear.

I once saw a cutt come half out of the water after a low-hanging bug. I hear about this happening all the time. Everyone has their stories. Fish come up on the bank, they break branches, they get caught briefly in the thick willow twigs before falling back into the river with a splash.

My best memory of a cutt crashing after a bug wasn't quite as impressive as any of these examples. It was most impressive because of the anticipation. My clients and I were floating under the Corwin Springs Bridge over the Yellowstone, and a client's errant cast shook a branch and dislodged a single Salmonfly, a big one. For whatever reason, the bug was unable to get airborne again. Maybe it was half-emerged, maybe it was injured by the fall. I don't know. Instead the fly drifted downriver in the mild chop for fifteen or twenty feet, no more than six inches from the bank. For much of this distance, there was little cover, and the bug drifted unmolested until it came to a dead, overhanging bush. No fly connected to a line could ever hope to follow the bug's drift, since there were far too many intervening branches. The bug was six inches from the bank, but six or seven feet up under the bush. The water under the bush was shallow, no more than six inches or so, and the bank was flat. Without overhead cover, no trout would be in water so shallow. With the shadows and protection provided by the bush, I just knew the bug was on borrowed time.

"Keep looking at that bug!" I said. "I guarantee it gets eaten." We were twenty feet away, not far beyond the bush, so when the green-gray dorsal fin of an enormous cutthroat broke water like that of a shark and a bulge of water arrowed towards the bug, I could see everything. The rise was so violent that the bush shook; the trout must have struck some its branches in its haste to eat the fly. In this moment, the trout was not concerned about being prey, it was not concerned about the numerous osprey that hunt this section of river. It was only focused on reaching its goal, just as the spawners concentrate on reaching theirs. Even if they do not know what this goal is, this quality can only be called bravery.

So it is really no surprise that Yellowstone cutthroats are considered poor fighters. Anglers pursue them after they have surmounted so many other challenges that they are exhausted. The female cutt I caught in Trout Creek is a prime example. She had ascended a cataract that would have its own state park in many Eastern states, only to encounter my fly. Hungry and exhausted, she ate it, only to find herself snared, rewarded for her fortitude with a hook in her lip. Many of her fellows, handled by less-experienced anglers or poachers, certainly fare far worse.

People have called me brave for descending into some of the canyons I regularly fish, or for scrambling through boulder fields where at times I've hurt myself. Maybe I am brave for doing these things, but I am not brave for fishing for cutthroats. I do not regularly consider the moral or ethical implications of trout fishing, and I am not going to do so here, but I will say this: the "challenge" of a smart cutthroat sipping Blue-winged Olive mayflies in Slough Creek or "winning the battle" with a cutt that does fight hard are nothing. The impressive thing is that the trout is there to be caught in the first place.

Hebgen Lake: Montana's Chub Hotspot

Author's Note: For whatever reason, I've never been able to get a magazine to bite on this short but punchy "how-to, where-to" article. I have no idea why...

When targeting chubs, there's nothing better than finding large numbers of good-sized fish close to the road. It's even better when the river or lake isn't crowded. The north shore of Hebgen Lake has both attributes, making it one of the best-kept chub secrets in the Rockies. The lake features an abundant population of Utah chubs from eight to fourteen inches long. One wonders why such a great fishery remains underutilized.

The peak of chub fishing in Hebgen is mid-June, when hundreds of thousands gather to spawn near the dam. At least I think they're spawning. It sounds accurate, right? The most effective method of finding chubs inshore is to be driving back to Gardiner, Montana from Reynolds Pass on the Madison River. Upon spotting hundreds of rolling fish you believe are rising trout, swerve into the first pullout you see and hop out almost before the car stops rolling. Odds are they're chubs.

Tackle requirements are simple. A five weight fitted with a floating line and a leader of any length tapered to whatever X will work in most situations. If it doesn't, so what? Your fly selection should contain a variety of wets and dries. Which? Well, that's probably up to you. Goddard Caddis, Griffith Gnats, Colonel Careys, Woolly Worms, and random goofy-looking wet flies I bought at a gas station while shopping for beer all work for me. Stripping wet flies is generally more effective than fishing dries, with fifty or sixty fish per hour possible (likely) when fishing subsurface compared to fifteen or twenty if you limit yourself to dries. I prefer Colonel Careys tied in a fit of traditionalism, flies which would otherwise sit in my box until they rusted and fell apart.

Hebgen Lake chubs prefer an active retrieve, meaning the best tactic is to cast to rolling fish or near cruising schools and to retrieve your fly quickly just under the surface. When targeting schools, most casts draw the attention of thirty to forty chubs at a time. Therefore, when you get a strike you should always use a strip set rather than set by lifting your rod, since a strip set allows a second fish to take if you miss the first. This process can be repeated as many times as necessary until you achieve a solid hookup.

One benefit of taking a chub fishing trip to Hebgen is the wide variety of other angling opportunities nearby. The Madison and Gallatin Rivers are both less than an hour away, and both feature excellent populations of whitefish. Many streams in nearby Yellowstone National Park also offer world-class whitefish angling. Most streams and lakes in Yellowstone Park also hold trout, for those so inclined. The Yellowstone River in Paradise Valley is within day-trip range, and the large suckers that call this river home make fine quarry, though they are more difficult to catch than the more-common and less-finicky 18-inch brown trout.

Fishing for Hebgen chubs is a special experience. The vast numbers of fish, the crash of seagulls seeking a meal, and the whoosh of cars on the road a few feet away all contribute to the experience. When he first experienced Hebgen's chub fishing, my friend Dave could only say "I feel dirty." With any luck, you will too.

Big Fish

Last summer I only fished Bear Creek once. Bear is probably my favorite of the Yellowstone's Black Canyon tributaries, since it's close enough to Gardiner to fish after I finish guiding or watching the fly shop for the day but remote enough that I can expect to be alone. The fishing is, of course, quite good. The creek produces mostly small cutt-bows, so it's not a secret hotspot, but I always enjoy myself while fishing it, so in a sense I feel like I ignored a friend by only visiting once.

My single trip was a good one, however, though it didn't start off that way. I rose only a single fish in the first fifteen minutes, a poor showing on a stream where I usually get at least ten six- to ten-inch fish an hour, with a twelve-incher thrown in once in a while for good measure. I was fishing a good section of creek, so I stuck with my initial fly—a brand new hopper I'd designed—for only a few pockets, thinking it might have been the problem, though I got the strike on it. The next pattern I tried was my standby #14 Coachman Trude, a pattern I like because it's highly visible and floats well, and because it has a body of peacock herl, which is a magic material. Nothing was interested in this fly, either.

Then I came to a long, deep pocket formed where three channels came together over a bottom of two slanted slabs of rock, and I found out where all the fish went. I think I caught eight out of this one pool, in maybe as many minutes. None cracked ten inches, but the whole point of the short three-weight rod and dry flies I was using was to let such small fish show their stuff. If I'd had my seven-weight and had been throwing streamers down in the big eddy pool where the creek hits the Yellowstone, I probably would have been disappointed. As it was, I was getting fish as big as I could expect and—all of a sudden— plenty of them.

After the big pocket, the afternoon turned around. A fish showed itself in virtually every eddy or pocket, and in a good looking stretch under an undercut lodgepole I actually saw a fish rising steadily, though I couldn't tell what he was taking. I raised him twice to the Trude in six casts, missing him each time, than got him to look at a Gray Wulff, which he didn't like as much. It seemed like the Trude was what he wanted, so I rested the fish for a few minutes and switched back. On my first cast I stung him for a moment before my hook pulled loose. He didn't look up again.

That fish stretched a good twelve or thirteen inches and looked like a pure cutt, if the flashes of him I could see as he rose were accurate. I figured I had just missed the fish of the day. It would have been more painful if it had been a twenty-four-inch brown in the Gardner, one of which I would lose in a more dramatic fashion a couple weeks later, but it hurt a little regardless of the fact that a twelve-inch trout is not a big one, at least to a human rather than a heron.

•

I'm not a saint, so all things being equal I'd rather catch big trout than little ones, but I'm also not the type of person who has to have big fish even if it means standing elbow to elbow with others, as it often is on some of the world's best rivers. Even the most crowded places in the Yellowstone region are never that bad, but some of them get pretty full. Instead of confronting crowds like Slough Creek gets in August, I'd rather stick to eight-inchers.

But when I am mostly fishing for small trout, an average-sized one can take on a whole new significance. While on Soda Butte Creek I might laugh if a twelve-incher rose to my fly, or in my darker moments be annoyed at it, especially if the drift was looking good and there was an eighteen-inch trout in the next lie downstream, on Bear Creek or the upper Gardner I'll take ten minutes out of my day to focus on one. Granted, I doubt I'll ever invest so much in any twelve-inch trout that losing it will break my heart as much as losing a five- or six-pound brown or a river cutt over twenty-two inches, but I am, after all, writing about a twelve-inch trout right now, and that must say something about the pull that a fish of moderate size can have on me, in certain situations.

The question than is, what defines these situations besides just the size of the fish? After all, I do catch twelve-inch trout on Bear Creek often enough that the loss of one shouldn't have stuck in my brain as it has. A big part of it is, I think, a shifting of desires and frames of reference to match the water, and thereby the fish, something some big-fish nuts are incapable of doing. Just as I switch to a light rod and dries to fish Bear Creek in order to best let its small trout show off, I must adjust my overall frame of reference. For an hour at least, the only fish I'm pursuing are six to eleven inches, with an occasional slightly larger one thrown in, so I must evaluate them within this framework. It's the same sort of process that allowed a nine-year-old client to proclaim "It's a big one!" upon catching an eight-inch brookie, when those he'd caught before had all been five-inchers. If the frame one is operating in doesn't include fish that are large in the grand scheme of fly fishing, a smaller fish will have to take over this role.

On the other hand, if the frame one is used to doesn't include small fish at all, it could be hard to get excited about the largest fish in Bear Creek. A few years ago I guided a couple kids from Alaska who were utterly disinterested in fishing dry flies to browns on the Gibbon River, since some of the trout they'd be catching were smaller than the bait they'd used for halibut up north. Their father had just been transferred from Juneau to Houston. I pity the poor kids.

Yet this idea of scaling desires to fit the water doesn't explain entirely why a given fish sticks in my brain more than another. There were certainly other memorable large fish I lost last season that have stuck in my brain, most clearly that big brown I mentioned a few paragraphs back, there are plenty of others I lost that didn't stick. I spent many more days on Soda

Butte Creek than I did on Bear Creek, losing many more large fish, but I can't think of a one as clearly as the twelve-incher on Bear Creek. Some of these Soda Butte fish were certainly difficult fish in tough lies, but amid the backdrop of all their fellows that I did manage to land, and the fact that somewhat large, somewhat difficult trout are the norm on Soda Butte, individual trout have faded to a montage of images blending together into the patchwork of memories that explain why I love to fly fish.

This suggests that I react to the size of a fish not only in terms of how it fits into its environment, but also how it does not. While the fish I lost on Bear Creek was a big one for its water, it wasn't out of the question, since I catch a twelve- or thirteen-inch fish every second or third time I visit the creek. Moreover, it was in exactly the right spot, in a sheltered nook under an overhanging undercut rootwad behind a rock. On Soda Butte, a spot like this would have nineteen-incher written all over it. A twelve-incher on Bear Creek is analogous to a nineteen-incher on Soda Butte, so that part of the equation adds up. Yet the fact that I spent ten minutes and went through two fly changes (even if the second change was back to the original fly) before managing to nick the Bear Creek fish was wildly unusual, considering that when fishing Bear Creek I usually use the same Trude all afternoon or until it falls apart, whichever comes first, and seldom bother casting to a spot more than five or six times before moving on to the next. Spending close to ten minutes and changing flies is more representative of the sorts of things that happen as a matter of course when trying for a wily old trout on Soda Butte.

With both the Bear Creek cutt and that big brown, most aspects of the situation fit perfectly with what I expect when I fish each river. On Bear Creek, the fly, holding water, and even the size of the fish weren't all that unexpected. It was the effort I put into getting him (or, in this case, not getting him) which made him seem big. In regards to that brown, everything about the flies I was using, the water I was fishing, and the effort I put into the single good strike were par for the course, yet the fish itself seemed out of place, since the average fall brown in that river is only sixteen to eighteen inches long and I've only caught a handful over twenty. The brown was much larger in absolute terms, and it was larger for its water than the Bear Creek fish, but I think of both of them as big trout, and I would have been thrilled to land either of them.

I have to admit that the thrill would have lasted longer with the brown.

Still, I would rather work hard for the occasional twelve-inch trout in Bear Creek than catch an infinity of large browns in a stocked pay-to-play creek, where the trout are stocked at lunker size rather than get that large the hard way. Some new anglers certainly don't see things this way, but most of us come to appreciate the surroundings and overall experience as much as the absolute size of a trout. This is one reason people from, say, Arkansas visit the Yellowstone area when all but the largest fish in Yellowstone would make decent appetizers for the world record browns in the Arkansas tailwaters. For that matter, if absolute size was a requirement, few people would fish for trout, especially with delicate little dry flies. Instead, bouncing doughballs on the bottom for carp and snagging paddlefish would be the sports of the intelligentsia. What all this suggests is that what I call a big trout, and maybe what most people call a big trout, is basically the same thing as what we call a "nice trout," a term less dependent on length and girth than it is on the quality of the experience and the effort put into it.

That could become a metaphor for something else, but I won't go there.

•

I tried for the nice cutt for a few more minutes, but I knew he probably wouldn't be back, so my heart wasn't in it. Eventually I continued on upstream, picking pockets as I had before stopping to concentrate on the cutt. I made my way quickly, as I usually do when fishing Bear Creek, and over the next half hour I mostly caught the usual eight- to ten-inch trout.

Then I reached a pocket where a bit of slower, deeper water ran alongside a log. Whatever had been hatching downstream wasn't coming off here, so there wasn't a rising fish in the pocket. I couldn't know for sure what kind of fish lived in the spot, but it was likely to be a big one. The lie was more exposed than the undercut lodgepole where the twelve-incher had been, but that lie had been close to perfect. This one was every bit as likely to hold a twelve-incher, since perfect spots are few and far-between on Bear Creek.

So I ran the Trude down alongside the log. Nobody home. On the next cast a five-incher swatted the fly at the bottom of the pocket, downstream of the log, a fish small enough that I derricked it in and sent it back on its way within fifteen seconds of the strike.

There really should have been something along the log, so I sent one more cast in tight to it. The third time was the charm. A fish casually emerged from a hollow between the bottom of the log and the rocks at the bottom of the creek, tilted up in the current, and sipped my large Trude like it was a tiny mayfly.

All this happened in less than a second, so I didn't consciously think about what I had become attached to until well after the hook was home, but when the fish turned and shot downstream out of the pocket and started pulling out line in little jerks, the images finally computed. This was no twelve-inch trout. It likely wasn't a fourteen-inch trout, either.

Most fish in Bear Creek take no more than a minute to land. This one took perhaps three, with me leaping from rock to rock downstream in a steeplechase routine to keep the fish from wrapping me around too many boulders. Eventually the fish came to a larger pocket, though, and I was able to get downstream of him, after which the outcome was no longer in doubt. The fish was huge, by Bear Creek standards, and unlike even the twelve-inchers, I didn't dare lift him by the fly to unhook it. Instead I maneuvered him into a small pocket against the bank, and got between him and deeper water. For the first time, I wished I bothered to carry a net on the creek, because though I'd stopped him, the fish still had quite a lot of fight, and despite my best efforts he managed to twist himself up in my tippet and batter himself against the bank before I could wet my hands and get him under control. Flipped over, the fish immediately calmed, so I was able to untangle the leader from around his body and get a good look at him for the first time.

The fish was a cutt-bow in true Bear Creek form, with the garish red stripe and spotting pattern of a particularly pretty rainbow and the golden hues and dark orange throat slashes of a male cutthroat just past spawning season. It was fat, too, as fat as an average Soda Butte trout, and longer. He measured sixteen inches exactly. I'd never caught a fish in Bear Creek larger than thirteen inches before. Now, my eyes have been opened to whole new possibilities. Could there be an eighteen-inch trout in the creek? Could one of the occasional small browns that find their way up into it get big enough to eat other fish, and keep growing until somebody caught it? Before, I wouldn't have entertained these thoughts. I thought I knew what to expect from the creek. Still, I can't let this single fish alter my idea of what to expect from Bear Creek, or it might be ruined for me.

Thankfully, I doubt this will be a problem. I yelled and carried on as I unhooked, revived, and released the sixteen-incher, but no louder than I had upon losing the smaller fish downstream, though the tone of my voice was happier and my language was slightly more polite. Even after releasing the larger fish, it still smarted that I'd missed the twelve-incher. Would I have traded them, rather caught the tough one and lost the big one I didn't spend many casts on? I don't know. I certainly know I'd like to see both of them again, though, since I think of both as big fish.

St. Francis River Goodbyes

The St. Francis River flows tannin-brown and swiftly from the mountains of the same name, and at Millstream Gardens Conservation Area cuts its way through a canyon walled by the oldest rocks in Missouri. These walls and scattered boulders of black granite were formed more than a billion years ago, when the name shared by river and range belonged not to a belt of hills only a little taller and steeper than most at the eastern edge of the Ozarks, but to a lofty mountain chain with newly-risen peaks still growing with continuous flows of lava.

The fish I sought when I last fished the St. Francis, before I left Missouri, could be relics of that time. Longnose gar scarcely seem a type of fish, but resemble instead aquatic dragons or young crocodiles, and they behave in much the same fashion. They rise to breathe air when the river does not carry enough oxygen, and cavort after schools of shad, tearing into them with beaks lined with hundreds of needle teeth, beaks too hard for a hook to penetrate. In late May they run upriver from the flatlands to the south, where the rushing river slows as it leaves the hills and enters the agricultural lands whose runoff turns its depths muddy and warm. When they run upriver they avoid the fastest currents, where the river flows in long runs of whitewater froth among the boulders, sometimes cutting many channels deeper than they are wide around the granite and through seams of softer stone, channels through which the kayakers of April cannot pass due to their narrowness. Instead they gather to spawn in the river's few pools, places where rock ledges meet the river in such a way that deep troughs are formed, or the river is half-dammed.

The best of these pools is a mile downstream of the nearest vehicular access, far from the trail hugging the second tier of bluffs. To reach the pool, one must slip and slide over the water-smoothed rocks, their surfaces marked by thousands of years of floods, fire, wind, ice, and rain. Along the way, small pockets of slow current hold smallmouth bass and sunfish large enough to cover a hand, though the 8-weight fly rod necessary to fight the gar does not allow these smaller fish to give their full measure, even when aided by runs into the relentless currents near their preferred lies, water whose character matches that of my favorite trout streams in Washington, Montana and northwest Wyoming, for which I would depart for good two days after my last trip to the St. Francis.

On my last trip I did not tarry long with the bass and bluegill, catching only a few of each as I made my way downriver, taking the largest bass from a sudden still spot downstream of a channel where the entire main flow of the river is compressed so tightly that a person only slightly more long-limbed than I could clear with a leap. Most days I would end at the best pool in late afternoon, switching from a 6-weight to the stouter rod only when I first cast to a sighted gar, but the pressures of packing and saying goodbye to friends who had not already offered me their best meant that I only had a few hours, and even this short trip threatened to be cut short by the thunderheads building in the northwest, visible between the pine-clad hills as they rushed downwind on a stiff, cool breeze. Though I would miss this river, I had no desire to extend my last day on it indefinitely by daring lightning while waving a 9'6" graphite stick. Thus, after only an hour of bass fishing I hurried downriver, climbing over and around hundreds of car- to house-sized rocks, skipping many pools and runs that had given up memorable bass over the years. The wet wind at my back pushed me towards the gar pools, towards the only Missouri fish I love that do not also swim in the rivers of the West.

I climbed over the last rocks unsure of what I would see. The pool could be still and empty save for the smallmouth and suckers hugging its bottom, or it could be a-boil with gar chasing shad and each other. Though I know that gar congregate in the pool, their comings and goings are almost a mystery to me. This time, after making my way past the drop that usually flips the kayakers who try it and around the slow, sandy eddy at the top of the pool, I was lucky enough to see the telltale ripples left by surfacing gar. There were many such marks, caused by the fish surfacing for air or chasing shad. In a few spots, the tips of their bills broke the surface, showing rows of teeth visible even from afar. There was nothing to do now but rig up and see if I could beat the storm now clearly rushing towards me. Already the sun had been covered by fast-flying cloud and the purple thunderheads looked ominous, though I could not yet hear thunder, due to the wind in the trees.

Gar will eat just about anything resembling a baitfish. Because of their hard mouths, the usual way of getting a gar on a fly rod is to lash a long hank of poly or soft nylon rope to a split ring or a large hook with the point clipped off, in the hopes that the tendrils of rope will tangle in the gar's teeth securely enough for the fish to be brought to hand. While my gar flies follow the same pattern, I make them more attractive than they need to be, tapering the strands of rope down the fly's body to give it a more realistic profile, tying in red feather gills and doll eyes, and coloring the white rope with magic markers to give it natural colors. When a fly of this pattern hits the water, it looks like it is swimming on its own.

I tied on one of the larger flies in my box, a fly as long and almost as wide as my hand, and cast it across and slightly upstream, so that the slow current would swing it down in front of the largest pod of gar. As the fly swung, I stripped it back in six-inch pops, so that it bounced in the water column and undulated seductively. Even in the flat light the white rope glimmered.

Over the next twenty minutes, I had three strikes and briefly "hooked" one fish. In each case, I failed to give the fish enough time to chew on my fly before lifting the rod tip, which meant that as soon as the fish realized something was amiss the fly came shooting back at me, having caught only a moment in the gar's teeth before pulling free. The storm was now bearing down on me, setting the trees atop the ridges thrashing in the violent gusts that did not quite make it down into the gorge. I figured I had another ten minutes, at most, before I would need to break down my rod and get under the bushes.

Then I felt another jolting take. I immediately dropped my rod tip and fed line, giving the gar time to entangle its teeth. When the slack started cutting upstream with a hissing sound, I lifted the rod and found I was fast to a fish. This time the fly held.

The fish ran hard upstream at first, then down. It jumped twice and tailwalked straight at me, before diving towards the jumbled rocks at the bottom, bulldogging. After three minutes of this the gar's head came up, and I was able to bring it to the surface, where it thrashed and thrashed until I drew it up onto a sandbar at the pool's head. The gar was maybe forty inches long and five pounds, about average for the St. Francis. Fat drops of rain were starting to fall, so I decided not to risk taking my camera out of its waterproof case and instead only cut apart my fly to free the fish. It swam off strongly, none the worse for wear.

I straightened and started to adjust my tackle to try for another, but as I was tying on a new fly the storm broke loose. In moments I was soaked to the skin and the hilltops vanished in the rain. Clearly this was a sign that one last gar should be enough, and it was.

The Tourist Trout

In some ways it seems like brown trout know they don't really fit in the Yellowstone drainage. Unlike brookies and rainbows, and unlike their own kind elsewhere in the Park, they live only in stretches of river where Yellowstone cutthroats were doing just fine without any competition from introduced species. Moreover, they spawn in fall, unlike the rainbows, which means that they cannot interbreed with cutts. Brookies spawn in the fall, too, but they vanish into headwater streams and so do their business out of sight and to a degree out of mind. In the past, some of the best spawning gravel the browns used was close enough to the road that tourists would get out to take pictures of them on their redds, or to hope for a shot of them ascending in flashes of silver through some of the Gardner's worst rapids, like salmon.

With their silver hues, large average size compared to the average local fish, and epic spawning runs, these fish are mistaken for salmon by a few tourists every season. Their confusion is not as foolish as it sounds. The brown trout that make their fall runs up the Gardner almost seem like different species than the resident browns, which wear chocalatey brown and butter yellow hues year round. The residents are Von Behr browns, from Germany, literally German brown trout; the runners are Loch Levens, from Scotland, fish descended from sea trout stocks. The fish that ascend the Gardner are the brown trout analogues to steelhead, save that they have long been divorced from the salt tang of the sea. Perhaps the hot spring discharges, rich in dissolved minerals including various salts, are what call them back to the river year after year.

So these are European trout living in a river where once cutthroats filled the riffles to spawn in the spring, but no longer. The Euro-fish must be neurotic in some ways. They wear hues that would better suit them in the icy waters of the North Atlantic and the peaty brown lochs through which their ancestors swam, seeking spate streams descending from the Highlands, flowing high and gray with the rains that saturate the moors in fall. Like their ancestors they spawn in October and November, but instead of the high, rain-swollen streams that provided protection for their great-grandparents eighty generations gone, they more often find the waters flowing clear and at close to their yearly lows, glassy enough to reveal them to any viewer, two-legged or four. While the native cutts and their long-lost Pacific coastal cousins the rainbows are wise enough to spawn under cover of the spring melt—the Rockies season most closely matching the fall spates of Europe—the immigrants continue their old habits, a relic of the Old Country not so suited to the new.

A habit carried over from their homeland that does suit them here is their wariness. Whereas cutts and rainbows were only occasionally netted or speared by American Indians, and were virtually ignored in the Yellowstone drainage, brown trout have been pursued on the fly for many centuries, perhaps even millennia. The philosopher and historian Ælian recorded an account of Macedonian anglers taking a peculiar spotted fish from the steep drainages of their mountain homeland, a fish that during certain periods refused worms and other live baits in favor of a reddish brown insect that emerged from the water in the spring. The Macedonians took their fish during these periods with a contraption of wool and gamecock feathers, fished with a six-foot rod and a line of the same length. Because of the shortness of their lines, they must have been fishing on or near the surface—they were dry fly fishing in 200AD. At any rate, all brown trout have been fished for hard and long for far longer than their American relations. Among all browns, those of the British Isles, targeted for centuries by members of the aristocracy who often had nothing to interrupt their trout fishing save salmon fishing and hunting, are perhaps those with wariness bred most-thoroughly into their genes.

Which means that the great silver browns that ascend the Gardner are seldom seen save in the fall. They come from nowhere, like apparitions. They don't really need an ocean to vanish into the protection of vast waters: the Yellowstone in which they spend most of the year is vast enough to shield them from the snares of all but the most skilled or the luckiest.

Thus the fish that come up the Gardner in the fall seem like many other short-term European visitors to Yellowstone. They seem out of place, they are nervous interacting with locals, they tend not to follow local customs, and they can act aggressively at times.

•

In the fall, this aggression can become almost comic. It is as though the brown trout throw aside all the care and caution that served them in the summer for an orgy of bloodlust. My friend Ranger Dave catches them on traditional Spey and Dee flies, giant Atlantic salmon and steelhead patterns. When he's not using his stonefly nymphs or his Bead, Hare, and Copper nymph, Matt Minch—who in all likelihood has fished the Gardner more days than anyone else ever will—uses a fly he calls a Creep, a size 4 streamer hook dressed with eight white rubber legs and a body of half black and half fire orange sparkle chenille. It looks like something you'd use in Alaska for spawning silver salmon, or maybe for largemouth bass. Matt catches plenty of rainbows on the Creep in addition to browns, but whenever the strike is so hard that his seven-weight rod almost jerks from his hand, he knows it's a brown.

Some of my top flies for the fall browns are only slightly less ridiculous. One of the less popular stonefly nymphs in the region that's still worth carrying is a black contraption with rubber legs, pearl Flashabou bound to the top of the body from tail to head, and a hackle about three times the size it should be. If I were charged with the task of creating a stonefly nymph with the proper coloration, segmentation, and tail of a Salmonfly just prior to emergence, but otherwise bearing the least possible resemblance to the real insect, this is the fly I would tie. I never fish them in the spring, when fully grown stonefly nymphs are actually a reasonable food source. In August through November, the period when there are least likely to be any full-size stonefly nymphs around, all of them having emerged and become winged adults the previous July, they are among my favorite flies.

Sometimes I even strip them back, like streamers. Stoneflies can't swim. It doesn't matter. The fish slam them anyway.

•

Some locals love browns, some hate them. Some people bear a curious mixture of these feelings. They love angling for browns, but kill as many as they legally can, which nowadays is unfortunately as many as they want, in the Gardner River if nowhere else. Since only a few hundred browns ascend the Gardner in any given year, this doesn't do much good for the population. I hate the people who kill vast numbers of browns, though it's okay to kill one or two a season.

That's how many I usually kill, or I should say "sometimes" kill. It's been a couple seasons since I popped one. When I do, I make a ceremony of it. I usually try to kill a male, since they convert less of their body mass into eggs and so taste better, and because males can mate with several females. I also try to kill my yearly fish early, in August or September, because a fish taken early is liable to have more meat on it than on taken late, because—like salmon—these fish do not eat on their spawning runs save out of aggression.

I try to keep an average-sized fish, one stretching sixteen or seventeen inches. A fish this size is big enough to make a meal on its own. After filleting the fish, I may do one of several things with it: I may roll it in a 50/50 mixture of cornmeal and Bisquick seasoned with salt and pepper, a recipe from my grandpa in which the proper amount of seasoning is "when you think you have enough, add some more." This is the way my dad almost always cooks trout. Sometimes I'll bake the fish in butter and lemon juice. Sometimes I'll poach it in butter, white wine, and lemon juice. Lately I've been grilling the one brown I keep, usually after marinating it in orange teriyaki sauce.

It seems appropriate, marinating a European trout caught in extreme northern Wyoming or extreme southern Montana not long before the snow flies in a sauce from Hawaii or the Far East that includes a summer-ripening fruit that doesn't grow within a thousand miles. Like the trout, it doesn't seem like it should fit, but also like the trout, in the end it all works perfectly.

Why I Hate Trout Lake

Trout Lake is something of a rarity in Yellowstone's northeast corner. While most of the rivers in the area, Soda Butte, the Lamar, and even the fast-flowing Yellowstone itself can be expected to pump out large numbers of fourteen-inch trout, with some occasionally cracking twenty inches, I've yet to meet someone who has gotten an honest twenty-four-inch trout from any of these streams. A few claim to have done so, but pictures reveal otherwise. Most trout anglers are used to catching ten- to fourteen-inch fish, and even a chunky eighteen-inch cutt looks like a five-pounder to somebody who doesn't catch many fish over fourteen inches. I don't mean to imply that an eighteen-inch cutt isn't a nice fish, especially when it comes up to a dry fly, but it is not huge, not a fish that would tempt someone to get it mounted.

Trout Lake can, however, produce more than its fair share of "Oh Shit!" fish, those that make even catch and release advocates pause a moment to consider how nice a good mount can look. Ten-pounders are caught with enough frequency that it's not beyond reason to daydream about getting one as you slog up the hill from the trailhead. Still, these fish seldom come, and even the slightly more reasonable twenty-four-inch six-pounder is rare enough that catching one suggests purchasing a Powerball ticket back in Gardiner might not be a dumb idea. These larger fish have seen everything both skilled fly anglers and hardware slingers can think to throw, and most of the time these fish laugh at everybody. Still, the average fish *is* a fourteen- to twenty-inch cutthroat or rainbow, nothing to sneeze at.

I'm perfectly happy catching these fish, the time or two a season I fish Trout Lake, and though I like rivers better than lakes, I have to admit that the lake is pretty with the mountains reflecting off its bowl-shaped surface. It's the people that chase the fish who bother me.

•

Trout Lake used to open on June 15th. Now it opens with the general park season, on the Saturday of Memorial Day Weekend. At this time the rest of the rivers across the north end of Yellowstone are often near peak flows for the year, with giant logs rolling downriver like the spears of the Trout Gods, to impale anyone stupid enough to try to fish. Even if they aren't that blown out, they're always gray-brown in color, high, and cold, perhaps fishable with big stonefly nymphs and streamers but not the picture postcard trout streams most fly shops want to put on their websites or most tourists want to fish. By contrast

Trout Lake is at its best right off the bat, and everybody knows it.

Which means that on the morning of the opener, unless the weather is bad, which isn't out of the realm of possibility at 7000 feet in the Rockies, a veritable hoard of anglers will descend on the Lake (after first ascending the steep but short trail) and start flogging it with spinners, spoons, damsel fly nymphs, midges, Woolly Buggers, and various other tools of the trade. All of this is fine in theory, considering that Trout Lake is a fairly large pond that could support probably 30-35 anglers without difficulty if they were spread equally around its perimeter and in belly boats within the lake itself. Since Trout Lake's resident fish tend to cruise rather than remaining in one feeding station as those in streams usually do, everyone should get a fair shot at the fish.

The problem is this: on the opener and for the month and a half of the season, 75% of the lake's adult cutthroats, the chunky fourteen- to twenty-inch fish the average angler is likely to catch, as well as a high percentage of the even larger pure rainbows, are stacked within twenty yards of the Lake's inlet creek or in the stream itself, spawning or eating eggs. The inlet is only about three feet wide, making it resemble an Alaskan salmon stream when a lot of fish are spawning, so it's sensibly kept closed.

The closure doesn't keep people from standing shoulder to shoulder just beyond the closure signs, bending the rules almost beyond recognition to justify casting their flies and lures into the area between the signs, but inches beyond the imaginary line drawn between the signs. Standing on the hillock above, it's possible to see dozens of large cutts jostling for position or spooking from getting lined or brushed on their dorsal fins by errant flies. Some of these fish range up to twenty-four inches, and most stretch sixteen inches or better. These are fully mature cutts, loaded with eggs and milt, eager to get on with their business. It looks like a hatchery raceway, since when most of the cutthroat in a three-acre lake are crowded into an area the size of a living room, individual fish don't have a lot of room to maneuver.

Watching those who stand just to either side of the signs, sometimes even leaning against they change flies or lures, I'm reminded of opening day at Bennett Spring, where I grew up fishing. Even back in Missouri, I hated the places and times where and when it was impossible to do anything but stand shoulder to shoulder, fishing for confused trout stocked that morning. The cutts are smarter, but they're just as vulnerable to getting snagged or stressed as hatchery trout, and the anglers who try for them usually have a better idea of how to catch trout than those who frequent the stocker streams in the Ozarks.

I fish Trout Lake maybe once a year, occasionally twice, and I might take a client to it once in a while, if the weather forecast calls for nastiness that will keep the crowds away, but though I might get down on my belly to take pictures of the spawners up in the inlet, spooky with not only their dorsal fins but also a third of their backs exposed above the water surface, I never fish next to the closure signs, and I usually don't let my clients stand alongside them, either. Despite these self-imposed limitations, we get more fish than the poachers and almost-poachers.

True, they average an inch or two smaller than those steeling themselves to run up the creek, since many are juvenile cutts. Still, there's something to be said for drifting a pair of midges under a tiny indicator along the drop-offs along the lake's steep north shore and picking up three or four fish an hour, or sometimes more, and not knowing whether it will be an eight-inch juvenile cutt or a twenty-seven-inch rainbow. Such possibilities tend to set the heart racing, especially when the little orange football indicator suspending one's flies skids a foot to the right and dives with authority. There's always that moment as you set the hook when you have no idea what you've gotten into.

All would be well, were it not for the hordes gathered around the inlet. I don't let my clients join them, but I tend to fish and have my clients fish along the north shore, within a hundred feet or so of the crowds around the inlet. The shore is steepest here, meaning that deep water can be reached with an easy roll cast. There are also several good points, making it possible to cover a wide variety of water from one casting position. Unfortunately, this shore is within sight and usually earshot of the inlet, and those casting over the backs of the stressed spawners always pay attention to every fish my clients or I hook, and especially notice our spontaneous shouts of happiness when one of these fish turns out to be a big one.

Nowhere else I guide or fish is the screech of a stressed drag a moment to dread, but when one of my clients or I hook a big fish, guys fishing around the inlet come running, especially those who have big fish on the brain from watching and casting over the spawners without any luck all morning long. One almost started a fight with me, in fact. I had two clients strung out over about 30 yards of the north shore, one at the first big point and the other on a smaller point about fifteen feet from the no fishing sign, which for once didn't have somebody fishing right by it. The wind was blowing hard from the west, so my client was casting at a 45 degree angle into its teeth, 180 degrees away from the closure, and letting his midges drift back to him. He missed several strikes while watching the large fish in the inlet through his polarized glasses, a common enough problem among clients and one I must admit to sharing. Then he caught a nice one, the first fish to be caught by anyone in view for almost an hour. An angler on the other side of the closure saw my client fighting the fish, then hot-footed it to our side. Even as I was releasing my client's fish the newcomer stopped five feet to our left, between us and the sign, and flung his spinner sidearm two feet out from the log and parallel to it, directly into the closed area.

"You can't fish there," I said, "Can't you see the sign? You have to cast away from the closed zone."

He said nothing, only reeled in quickly and cast a foot or two from my client's strike indicator.

"Come on man, it's a big lake. You don't have to crowd us. Why don't you go back where you were?" My voice had risen several decibels.

He reeled in again, but this time he rounded on me. "I don't want to start anything with you, but I'm going to if you don't shut up."

I don't remember what I said next, but it was a variation on the same theme, plus a note that he could cover a lot more water with spinning tackle than my client could with fly gear, so ought to give us some space. Either I was a lot more persuasive this time or the guy really didn't want a confrontation, despite his big talk, because he went back around to the other side of the inlet and started crowding the people on that side, which wasn't what I'd meant for him to do.

Of course, the stereotype of spin fishermen suggests they're supposed to be louts, but many of the fly anglers who try for Trout Lake's fish are no better. On shore they give each other enough space, if for the simple fact that it would be impossible to cast effectively otherwise. The real banes of my shore-bound clients are the float tubers. Tubes help a lot on the lake, since they allow an angler to cover whatever portion of the lake he wants, including the steep, wooded south shore that holds some big fish and is impossible to fish on foot because of the trees. One would think that tubers would patrol this shore, or would troll along some of the ledges and weed beds near the middle of the lake, but early in the year many only use their tubes to get at the spawners from the deep water side. From thirty feet out in the lake, they can see everything when one of my midging clients gets a fish without even turning their heads.

On the plus side, it's a lot easier to let a tuber know they're too close than it is to tell a bank angler the same thing; one only need cast within a few feet of the tube. A #22 Zebra Midge dropped below a #18 Lightning Bug doesn't make the point with as much authority as a big tunghead Woolly Bugger, but it's still fair notice that a tuber is invading your space. Sometimes they don't get the message, though. Once a troller cruised right in front of us, and my client didn't even have to alter his casting pattern to let his flies drift within two feet of the guy. He paddled within 30 feet of us, through water my client had been fishing for the past half hour. Instead of taking the hint, he only scowled at us and kept stripping his damsel nymph.

"Would you mind giving us some more space?" I called out, after he turned around and started trolling back along about the same route. "You've got the whole lake if you want it!"

"I want this part of it," he said, and kept on trolling. Confronted with this sort of attitude, my client and I packed up and headed over to the Yellowstone River in the lower Grand Canyon. He was hoping for bigger fish than the Yellowstone can reasonably be expected to provide, but he said he'd rather have twelve-inchers in nice surroundings than deal with assholes.

And that's what it comes down to, really. Yellowstone is known rightly as one of the greatest trout fishing destinations on the planet, and it provides the largest concentration of public water in the Lower 48. Yet so many people seek only the famous water, obsessed with the idea of a big fish or even just a big hatch, that many of Yellowstone's fisheries are just as crowded as anything back east. One of the products of such crowds is irritation, with people getting stressed out and angry at each other, and thinking that they have to protect their turf, as though others are somehow stealing their fish. If visitors want to feel like that on their vacations, fine. After all, people from New York or Boston are probably used to it. They might be more stressed by fishing a creek or pond that didn't call for stress than by dealing with a crowd similar to those at home, even if they're not consciously aware of it.

That's fine. Most of the people who come to Yellowstone visit once a year for a week or so, and after all I make my living taking some of them fishing. If some visitors would rather elbow people out of the way like they do back home, they're welcome to it. I moved west partially because rivers in Missouri were too crowded for my tastes, especially its limited trout streams, and I have no interest in embracing the stress that such crowded conditions cause. I'll continue to fish Trout Lake a time or two per season, and I'll bring my clients there when they just have to have a shot at a big fish early in the season, but I'll try not to get very worked up about the place. The lake itself is beautiful in its wooded bowl in the mountains; that's not the problem. I don't really hate the lake itself, I hate the people that crowd around it looking for big fish, and when I stand on the steep north shore midging or creeping a damsel nymph along the bottom and scream at anybody who comes too close, I turn into one of them. If it doesn't make sense for somebody to come to Yellowstone and stand in a crowd, it really doesn't make sense for someone who moved to the area to get away from crowds to do the same thing, and get irritated at himself and those around him in the process.

North Fork Portrait

When Scott and I arrived at the North Fork, the air was redolent with the scent of evergreens and the fertile stench of decay. Firs, spruces, and hemlocks stood all around us, but the explanation for the other smell was not apparent until we walked out on the little Forest Service bridge over the river. The good pool beneath it was full of salmon.

Most of the fish were pinks, fish of sixteen to perhaps twenty-five or twenty-six inches, a pound and a half to six or seven pounds, but scattered among them were vast chinooks, some easily going twenty pounds or more, dark shadows hovering over the bottom, leviathans in this easily-waded mountain river. It was an idyllic scene, a reminder of the runs that filled all the West Coast rivers before humans disrupted the runs in our idiocy. But down among the fish was a spot of brightness, a flash of metal out of place among the migratory fish. Scott, more eagle-eyed than I, squinted and said, "It's a damn Buzz Bomb."

The scene was ruined. Buzz Bombs, heavy vertical-jigging lures, are meant to be fished in deep water out in Puget Sound. In a steep mountain river like the North Fork, full of pocket water and ledge pools, it was as out of place as a refrigerator tossed in the river. That is, if the angler actually expected a fish to bite. As a snagging tool, cast over the backs of closely-packed salmon and retrieved with quick sweeps of the rod tip to hook fish in the back or side, it made perfect sense. Some people just need to ruin Paradise.

Since the pool below the bridge was too deep to wade out and retrieve the Buzz Bomb, litter in the worst sense of the word, there was nothing to do but rig up—for bull trout, not salmon, which cannot be legally targeted in the North Fork, by fair means or foul. Scott chose a black rabbit strip sculpin and I a red and white articulated Bunny Leech on one rod and an egg and a flesh fly on the other. I almost always carry a light rod for nymphs and a big one for streamers on the North Fork, loving the flexibility provided by carrying two rods even while despising the pain of transporting the spare.

We headed upstream along a narrow track kept open by the few anglers to visit this remote, not particularly productive stretch of river and by the hikers who come to view the waterfall at its head, the definitive limit to upstream migration for anadromous fish like the salmon, bull trout, and occasional steelhead. The trail wound through red cedars and firs, past dense stands of blackberry shrubs and devil's club, before descending to the river perhaps two hundred yards upstream of the bridge. The river was split into two channels. One of them held a good pool, a pool where I had taken sea-run cutthroat and bull trout, and where a friend of Scott's had once taken an extremely dark but unspawned seventeen-pound winter steelhead in July, months after it should have finished spawning and returned to the sea.

The pool and the other channel, which was mostly just a shallow riffle, were now full of salmon. Many pinks and chinooks rested in the pool, both in its gut and its tailout, and over against the tangle of logs on the far bank. As I watched, one of the dark kings rolled, throwing up a great splash. Pinks thrashed their way up the shallow channel, coming almost completely out of the water in their haste to ascend to the micro-pool above the next series of boulders. Few of these fish save those that hung over a pair of redds in a deeper spot bore the fungus usually worn by spent salmon, and some were quite bright considering that pinks usually begin to turn as soon as they enter fresh water, but many of them bore scars, earned by fighting their way up similar shallow channels, mile by mile.

With so many salmon crowding the pool it seemed unlikely we would find any bulls in it, and we did not. Scott and I both slung our streamers over towards the logs, retrieved them jerkily, imitating a wounded sculpin or, perhaps in this water, an injured chinook smolt. Then I drifted the egg up under the logjam, losing one fly. One of the pinks chased Scott's streamer for a moment before he noticed and picked the fly up, to avoid hooking the fish, but that was the only interest shown to our flies here, so we moved on.

It went much like this for the next two hours, save that in the third pool we each caught a pair of miniature whitefish on egg imitations. We saw no more chinook, but pinks filled this pool as well, some resting in the gut of the run, some hurrying upstream towards the next rapid and the pocket water beyond.

Beyond this pocket water, in a tight little run with a hard current tongue against the far bank and a narrow slot of bottomless green water on our side, tight to the rounded boulders, Scott finally picked up a bull trout, a thirteen-incher, a fish that smashed a woolhead sculpin half its size. I have a picture of Scott releasing this fish. It looks ludicrous, a child's drawing of a fish eating a fly, the proportions all wrong. Still, it was a fish.

The salmon must not have liked this pool, because a few minutes later I got a bull trout just downstream of where Scott caught his. This was a better fish, not huge, but strong and fat, and though it came from a pool where the pinks had pushed it rather than from a pool where there were actually any spawning salmon, it ate a pink egg with a red dot. It ate hard enough to drag my strike indicator a foot under. In the fast current rip, fighting against my 6-weight and a comparatively webby tippet, the fight was nip and tuck, the fish bulldogging along the bottom. At my shout Scott came running, though he could only stand by as I slipped down from the boulders into waist-deep water to land the fish. It went eighteen inches, about average for bull trout in the North Fork. We were hoping for bigger fish, of course, but a few more of these would do.

For me at least, it was not to be. We fished upstream through one more pool filled with pinks and a single, solitary, battered chinook, then worked up through the steep stretch of pocket water that tumbles for two or three hundred yards below the falls. I had never gone all the way to the falls, and since the river was low enough to make reaching the falls easier than usual, I decided to make the scramble. I enjoy scrambling over water-worn rocks, especially sliding down the larger ones to fish new pockets, but today I made my way quickly upriver rather than messing with the pocket water. Bull trout do not like to hold in pocket water, and the chances of a summer steelhead in the North Fork are so minimal that I didn't bother spending much thought on the idea. Still, one of the three summer-runs Scott had taken from the river, all hatchery strays, had come from just under the falls, so I would fish the plunge pool there hard, trying to pay attention to my flies as well as the pretty waterfall.

I saw no pinks on the trek, and only a single fish, which I caught. I stopped to run my egg pattern down a deep slot a hundred yards below the falls, a deep run that just shouted "steelhead." On the first drift, my indicator dived hard. I set, heart leaping, brain shouting *This is it!* The fish made one headshake, and then I knew that I had found no steelhead. In thirty seconds I brought in the fish, a resident rainbow trout. The fish was beautiful and thirteen inches long, but I could not help but feel that it was somewhat anticlimactic. With the way the indicator went under, I had been certain I was into a steelhead.

The falls roared, sending out gouts of spray that made me glad I'd thrown on my rain jacket despite the blue of the afternoon. The force of the fall's descent sent random gusts of wind swirling downriver, buffeting me and slicking back the wisps of hair that stuck out from beneath my hat. Downriver boulders predominated, but under the wind- and waterfall-whipped waves coming from the base of the fall, I could see otherworldly sculptures of solid bedrock, or more likely here in the Cascades, lava. Like the Yellowstone I fish so often, the falls on the North Fork must have been created where the river intersected a soft seam of lava rock and continuously ate away at it, causing a notch. Or so I reasoned as I stood atop one pinnacle of water-sculpted rock, looking down into the green depths beneath the fall.

My flies never found bottom in this pool, even when I switched to my heaviest sink-tip to probe for bull trout that might be prowling beneath the hundreds of salmon that milled about the great pool as if unsure what they should do now, having found their way upriver abruptly blocked. I hooked one fish, a pink, which for whatever reason decided that the bunny strip flesh fly I fished ahead of an egg looked like food. Perhaps it triggered a memory of herring, or perhaps the fly was only in the right place at the right time. Or the wrong place. Unlike the snagger who'd left his Buzz Bomb in midriver, I had no interest in disturbing the salmon and shook my rod tip until the barbless hook came lose. After this I stumbled my way across the waist-deep tailout at the bottom of the plunge pool, every bit of exposed skin soaked and hem of my jacket sodden by the waves scudding across the surface.

By now Scott had reached the waterfall pool and probed its depths with a streamer, as I had already tried. He likewise caught nothing. I explored the other side, where the water-twisted rocks were distorted into still more fantastic shapes, like melted plastic turned to stone. I slipped and slid among the rocks, and in a nook beneath the fall I looked down through twenty feet of water, all filled with pink salmon. I did not bother these fish, only watched them as I cast my egg and flesh fly into the current seam created by the force of the fall, where there weren't any salmon. I paid more attention to the fish I could see than the flies which might draw unseen trout.

After a half hour of probing the plunge pool, the largest pool on the entire North Fork, Scott and I turned downstream. In a pool we had both bypassed on our way to the fall, a pool free of salmon, Scott spotted a long gray-purple shadow laying on the bottom as though asleep. Longer than a pink salmon, too short for a chinook, and too dark to be a summer steelhead, this had to be a bull trout, and a big one.

Scott had spotted the fish, so he got the first shot. He swung his Double Bunny inches from its nose a dozen times, not sparking even a moment's interest. He was about to turn away in frustration, to give me my shot, when from the shadowy boulders on the other side of the river, against a rock wall, where we could see nothing, a long dart shot from its sheltering stones, enraged at the fly or maybe the reticence of its companion in the pool to take advantage of the easy meal. The fish Scott had been targeting moved at last, panicked by the coming of the unexpected bull trout, but neither of us paid it any mind as it darted off. The other fish was just as big, and it took in a rush.

Scott, more used to large, sea-run fish than I, fought the fish harder than I would have thought possible, preventing it from running upstream or down. At times he even slid his reel hand far up the rod, to provided additional leverage, bending the stiff Loomis rod in a steep curve, until it was almost a half-circle. Under this much pressure, the trout could only bulldog, rubbing its snout along the cobble bottom in an attempt to free itself. To no avail. After a sharp, brief fight, Scott waded out and knelt, and tailed the fish.

It was the largest bull trout I'd yet seen, though by no means an exceptional one for this river. It was twenty-four or twenty-five inches long, five pounds perhaps, of mixed purple and green hues fading to silver and white on its belly. Looking now at the photo I took, when Scott lifted the fish only long enough for me to snap the shot, briefly enough that the drops of water did not have time to fall from his cradling hand or the trout's fins, I am struck by how the film of water around the bull's body makes it seem to glow.

After releasing the fish Scott secured the Double Bunny to his hook keeper and grinned. He would later estimate that this single fly would take forty bull trout and a couple unexpected, unsought coho salmon over a dozen trips before it began to fall apart, statistics that would earn it a treasured place on his wall of retired flies.

We continued downriver, ready to call it a day. We passed the pools filled with chinooks and pinks struggling upriver, and the run where the trail from the parking lot came down. Scott, still excited by his catch, suggested we continue down to the bridge, looking for a last fish. We saw no more bull trout, and save for a moment of excitement when we spotted what we took to be a steelhead lying in a tailout, we saw no fish we cared to pursue. The possible steelhead turned out to be a chinook, still silvery-bright and robust despite the lateness of the season; only its slightly worn tail kept me from thinking it a steelhead and casting to it. And that was it for the fishing. After passing the chinook, I broke down my rod. Scott, still hopeful, left his rigged until we passed under the shadow of the bridge.

At the head of the last pool there was a backwater that purled softly against the roots of the undercut red cedars. It was dark under the shadows of the trees, and a few willow leaves that had turned golden earlier in the season than most swirled just under the surface, waterlogged. That's why we didn't see the old pink until we almost stepped on it.

The fish lay on its side among the fallen leaves. Unlike its brethren resting in the pools or struggling upstream through the riffles, this one had already spawned. It was a female, easy to recognize as such by the delicate swelling over her back rather than the grandiose hump the males carry. She was battered, and her flesh hung from her in long strips. A white coating of fungus covered her from head to tail. It human terms, she was ugly, but then again most people consider all pink salmon ugly.

It took a moment to see the gentle waves lapping from the spent hen salmon's gills as she breathed. We had thought her dead, since she did not react when we approached. She soon would be, like the leaves she lay among. Somewhere upstream there was a redd well-filled with eggs, to make the next generation that would return to this high stream in the Cascades in two years' time.

Scott crouched next to the dying fish. "You did good work, girl," he said. "Rest now. Rest now."

The Jeweled Trout

Richard Parks, owner of Parks' Fly Shop, is fond of describing what he'd do if he were to invent or otherwise get his hands on a time machine. The first thing he'd do would not be to go back and stop John Wilkes Booth or to witness some profound moment in history, though he might well do these things later. He wouldn't even go back and punch in some Lotto numbers for a huge jackpot for which he'd be the sole winner.

No, he'd do something only a Yellowstone-area fly fisherman would do. He'd put an end to our speculation and whining about how good the upper Gardner would be if it were originally stocked with cutthroat from Slough Creek. He'd grab Captain Boutelle by the lapels and scream in his face to do this, and failing that, he'd bring the shell-shocked former Commissioner of Yellowstone Park to the future and show the man who stocked Yellowstone seemingly at random what he had wrought in the formerly fishless but ripe upper Gardner: a river system of long hairpin bends and fishy riffles, of deadfall trees and undercuts, of creeks that see dense hatches of Green Drakes, Yellow Sallies, Pale Morning Duns, and several species of caddis, all of which are eaten by brook trout averaging seven or eight inches in length instead of Slough Creek-origin cutthroat averaging fourteen. Oh, what could have been.

I'd do the same thing as Richard. Yet Richard and I both spend a lot of time with our three-weights and dry flies, stalking the Gardner above Osprey Falls, Lava Creek, Blacktail, and all the other creeks and small rivers where brookies are the only trout. Brookies in Yellowstone are a paradox: most locals would happily replace them in most streams with big cutts, or in some misguided cases with rainbows and browns, but at the same time many brookie streams get fished rather hard, sometimes in order to teach kids to fly fish, sometimes just because you can usually be alone on them and dry flies are almost always the ticket.

And unlike cutthroat water, most locals who are really into the sport have a few secret brookie spots up their sleeves. I have a couple cutt spots and a few more where the early fall-run browns stack up, but my brookie honey holes are even more numerous— assuming it makes any sense calling a spot where the fish might max out at a foot rather than ten inches a honey hole.

I'll share one, considering it's not really a secret. Joffe Lake is a little pond near Mammoth that's chock full of brookies. In years past it was hard-pressed to put out a fish over eleven inches, but this year it's pumping out some surprisingly large fish. The reason isn't entirely clear, but around the shop we have a working hypothesis: the lake is manmade, serving as a regulating reservoir for the Mammoth water supply reservoir uphill, so its inflow tends to go up and down depending on Mammoth's water needs. Last year, there must have been a problem with the uphill reservoir, requiring its outflow to be shut down for a week or ten days, or maybe the Park Service just wanted to fill it quickly. Joffe, being something of a redheaded stepchild, didn't receive its usual share of new water for over a week, while its own outflow pipe remained hard at work, sending Joffe's water down into the Gardner at the bottom of Sheepeater Canyon. The lake lost maybe a quarter of its total volume, but probably half its surface area, because much of the lake has a shallow bottom. There's a bay at the north end of the lake which is one of my favorite spots. The brookies dart from the weeds along its bottom to take scuds or small, bright streamers during most of the season, but last year it was completely dry.

This meant that the poor stunted brookies were packed into a much smaller area than usual, with less food, more chance of contracting the trout version of the flu, and a better chance of getting eaten by an osprey or mink. We think many of them didn't make it, leaving plenty of room and plenty of food for the survivors, especially since the lake's re-flooded margins received an increased nutrient load from the decay of young terrestrial plants that started to colonize the lakeshore.

At any rate, there are a handful of twelve- to fourteen-inch brookies in Joffe, and probably a dozen or two up to sixteen or seventeen. There are plenty of eleven-inchers, keepers that go great with teriyaki sauce and a medium-hot grill

Most visitors to Yellowstone don't think twice about keeping a brookie, either for the grill or the frying pan. Maybe it's because they are so small and there are so many of them, or maybe it's because they taste so damn good when they're fresh. Either way, they're what amounts to the official food fish of Yellowstone. Nowadays you can keep as many as you want anywhere in the Park, and I know quite a few people who do so on a regular basis. I'm not really one of them, but I do kill three or four a few times a season. Like the bluegill of my youth, they're beautiful when they're alive, glowing with subtle iridescence, and like bluegill they're delicious. Both fish have a more delicate flavor than their larger cousins, with a hint of sweetness. I've noticed that most species that have evolved to never grow very large, breed prolifically, and die in vast numbers when young taste something like this. It doesn't make much sense, but perhaps Nature made animals that need to be eaten by many larger, more aggressive critters (including people) taste good, just so we'd keep their populations in check. Or perhaps we think they taste good for the same reason—Nature needed us to do a job, so made our taste buds tingle at the aroma or taste of a fresh brookie, rabbit, or quail. We may just be bees high on the scent of something other than a flower.

•

Brookies don't just taste something like bluegill, they sort of act like them as well. Like bluegill, I've always caught more brookies with something gaudy than with something that actually imitates the food available. In lakes, I usually fish a Joffe Jewel, a pattern developed for the lake by Matt Minch. It fits the same niche as a small Mickey Finn, and takes about three seconds to tie. It has a tail of red hackle fibers, a body of embossed silver tinsel, and a sparse wing of yellow over white marabou. That's it. Most of the lakes where I fish this fly don't have any minnows at all, with all the small fish being brookie fry, but even the few lakes that do have baitfish populations certainly don't have any gaudy yellow, red, and white ones. The brookies don't care. The two largest brookies I've ever taken from Joffe Lake both ate this fly.

In rivers, I use a half-dozen or so patterns, if only for sake of variety. My favorite fly of all is probably a #14 Peacock Caddis, mostly because it works well fished skated, cutting a wake, even during mayfly hatches when the bugs themselves absolutely don't do this. The fish don't care: they often throw themselves clear of the water in their haste to grab the fly. I often laugh when they do this, especially when the fish is as long as my finger and therefore can't even get the bug in its mouth, only holds it briefly, spins a flip in midair due to the weight of the fly and leader, and comes unbuttoned to splash back in the creek.

One of the reasons the Peacock Caddis seems to work so well is because of the body material that makes up part of its name, its thick, full body of peacock herl. No caddis has a body so fat, but this doesn't matter. Peacock herl is just magic, and the two quintessential brookie patterns both feature a peacock body. Anyone who has ever fished with Richard Parks knows which patterns I'm about to mention, and they're among my favorites, as well. I'm talking about the Coachman Trude and the beadhead Prince.

I fish Trudes and Princes in a wide variety of water, for every trout species that swims in Yellowstone Country. Trudes are among my best dries on the Yellowstone River, particularly early in the summer and in the middle of winter, while Princes are a good bet in any moderately fast or pocket water stream with caddis and stoneflies, ranging from trickles that descend from the high country at a forty-five-degree angle to the Yellowstone itself. Cutts love them, browns love them under the right conditions, rainbows tend to prefer the Trude to the Parachute Adams during some fall Blue-winged Olive hatches, and I've even been surprised by a six-pound sucker that decided to eat my beadhead Prince while I was fishing for runner browns in the Gardner.

Yet no species of fish so universally love the Trude and Prince (often fished together) as brookies. I won't fish a Prince in Slough Creek or lower Soda Butte, and though I may try a Trude as a strike indicator on lower Soda Butte when I'm using a small, invisible emerger or if I'm fishing a caddis hatch just before dark (and catch fish on it during these circumstances), it's not a go-to fly. Likewise, though I use the Peacock Caddis on rivers that have fish other than brook trout, I've yet to try it on a lake, since its excellent floatation makes it hard to fish the fly subsurface. When chasing brookies, I'll use the Trude and Prince anywhere, in any water type, using any retrieve, no matter what's hatching. Take a recent trip to some spring holes in the Gardner drainage, for example. There were some size-18 black and cream midges hatching, and every minute or two a brookie would boil after an emerging midge. Most of these trout were typical to the area, measuring ten inches or so, though they were fat on the spring holes' bounty, but some of these fish went fifteen or sixteen inches. No matter how big they were, the way to catch them was to cover the rises I saw with a #16 Trude squeezed wet, stripped just under the surface as fast as I could manage. It was great fun.

Both the Trude and the Prince are great beginner flies, and of course brookies, since they are the bluegill of the trout world, are great beginner fish. For one thing, the Trude has a dense, white wing that even the most visually-challenged client can see, provided he or she has taken my advice and bought a pair of polarized glasses for the trip. Even if they haven't, I can usually stand beside them and scream "STRIKE! STRIKE! STRIKE!" when a fish eats the Trude or it hesitates, signifying a take on the Prince. The Trude floats well, too, of course, with its dense front hackle and hair wing, especially when I dip it in Magic Sauce, the probably-toxic dry fly floatant Richard Parks manufactures in his shop's bathroom in gallon-jug lots. This helps it stay up during the dreadful drifts created for it and its usual #16 Prince dropper companion by rookie clients, when there's drag on the water, bellies downstream, and so on, which generally make the fly cut a wake through the river that would terrify most trout.

The brookies love it.

They'll even take when the fly is cutting a wake without even moving. If the unthinkable happens and a beginner client hasn't landed a single brookie with the guide trip almost over, a good thing to do is find a likely-looking riffle and stick my client just above the most likely-looking spot, then have him or her swing the Trude and Prince down into the best holding water and just hold the flies there. Eventually, though the dragging Trude and Prince look like nothing a fish in a river should eat, usually a brookie will just get so fed up after a few minutes that it will annihilate one or the other. On occasion, this commotion causes a second fish to attack the second fly, which always excites our clients. Two fish on one cast? Impossible!

A brookie that took a Trude or a Prince looks appropriate in the hand as it is readied for release. The trout wear hues of shimmering green, with highlights across the entire spectrum, and the peacock herl bodies of the flies, usually reinforced with fine gold wire, seem to amplify and reflect the color of the trout. When you open your hand and let the fish slip away, with the fly held an inch away from the trout between the other hand's index finger and thumb, the fish darts off, sending a shower of silver water from where its tail threshes air and water. Thus the emerald trout departs in a spray of silver water, reflecting golden sunlight and golden tinsel. It is difficult not to admire this sight, even if sometimes we wish it were not so common in what could be hallowed waters, rather than the place where we go when we want to catch a few easy brookies and relax. Of course easy fish and relaxation sure have their merits.

Latin

Occasionally someone asks how the larger of Parks' Fly Shop's boats, the *Aurigae Trudii*, got its name. This isn't my story, save that I tell it when asked about the boat, or when I have a client who will appreciate it. It happened sometime in the 1980s, on the upper Yellowstone River, where the wind sometimes whistles upstream so hard that the boat skates against the current, back towards the put-in.

•

The two sports were dressed to the nines, with the latest required technical angling wear, all the gadgets, and the neoprene waders that were still the cutting edge back then. Their rods were the best, of course, and fly boxes stuffed with everything they might conceivably need anywhere in the country bulged from their vests. If beadhead nymphs had existed then, they'd need a backpack to carry just their nymph boxes, but since weighted and unweighted nymphs were the two versions anybody had thought up yet, their vests were just shy of the breaking point. I'll call the sports "Doug" and "Ernie," because these two were inflexible acolytes of the two most-famous hatch-matchers of the day. Like most converts, these guys were way more serious about their new religion than the religion's founders.

I imagine they were a bit put off by the smallness of Parks' Fly Shop, and the simplicity of its fly selection. Where were the Crazy Charlies and tarpon patterns? No full-dress Atlantic salmon patterns? What did we mean, No-Hackles floated so poorly they were worthless?!

"What hatches can we expect tomorrow? I understand the *Pretensia* and *Verbosia* are hatching on the Yellowstone this time of year," one of them managed at last. Clearly, this was not the sort of place nor—seeing Richard, in his frumpy polo shirt and "well-aged" slacks—the sort of guide they expected.

Richard, who still calls Pale Morning Duns "little pale mayflies" and Green Drakes "big dark mayflies," scowled. "Well, there might be a few little tan caddis stumbling around in the afternoon, but we'll probably be fishing a Trude all day long."

These days about half of the shop's flies are custom-produced. I tie some, Matt Minch ties some, several of the shop's other guides tie some. We're all innovative tiers, and tying something that's just a *little* different is often just the ticket. There's also the cachet of a "custom" fly versus one mass-produced somewhere in the Third World. But this story took place years before I started guiding, indeed before I even started fly fishing. Going back in time, you'd pass a period where most of the shop's flies were manufactured overseas (as the vast majority of flies these days are), with a few by Matt Minch, and eventually come full circle, to a period where most of our flies were produced in-house, in this case matching Richard and his father's ideas of what a fly should look like. The story I'm relating here took place in the waning years of this first period.

So picture the Trude Richard would have pointed out. It would have been tied on a #12 Mustad 94840 hook, the default dry fly hook until the Japanese started making hooks that came out of their boxes sharper, lighter, more expensive, and trendier. We still stock Trudes tied on a hook with the same taper. This is where the similarities end.

Our contemporary Trudes are tied by either the Montana Fly Company or River-Run, Dan Bailey's import arm. Both of these are large-scale wholesalers, so their flies need to appeal to fly shops and subsequently fly shop customers throughout the United States and Canada. Therefore their Trudes are trim, pretty little things with a tail a bit shorter than the hook shank, a wing of tightly-packed fine white calftail stretching to about the midpoint of the tail, and two hackle feathers with barbs just a bit longer than the hook gape, wound on the front third of the hook shank.

The Trudes Richard used to tie for the rough and fast Yellowstone, the canyon stretch of the Gibbon River, and the steeply-tumbling Gardner don't look quite so trim. Their tails are one and a half times as long as the shank, their wings are much denser than the imported flies and almost reach the end of the tail, and their hackles are almost twice the gape of the hook. Except for the body, which is about the same as those on the production Trudes we sell now, one of Richard's #12 Trudes looks like someone else's #8.

I can only imagine the horror. *What could such a monstrous bug possibly imitate?* the sports would have wondered. A moth? A baby muskrat? The beauty of the Trude is that it matches nothing, so fish in fast-flowing water can take it for whatever they want. Peacock herl is iridescent and a white wing looks like it's in motion when viewed against the sky from below, so the Trude looks alive, even if it does not look like any real insect. Since Yellowstone River trout see a wide variety of hatches, but small numbers of most of them at any one time, and these hatches are usually mixed, a general pattern with a proper silhouette and suggestive qualities, but tied big to stand out, is usually more effective than a precise imitation.

Ernie and Doug couldn't handle it. All the books they had read told them that you have to match a hatch to catch more trout. They left the shop shaking their heads, already dreading the upcoming trip. It was far too late to cancel without losing their deposit, but clearly the local Yahoos they'd be going out with the next day were not up with the current science of fly fishing. Like most locals, they thought, they were in a backwater. It was too bad, too, because they'd heard the *Pretensia* hatch could be amazing.

•

Doug and Ernie had booked two boats, one for each of them. They'd read in the magazines how the person in the bow had things marginally better than the person in the stern, and since they were selfish misanthrope bastards with money they figured that each should get to be in the front all day long, rather than switching out at lunchtime, as most parties do.

Forget "sharing the experience," which is a lot of the fun for most parties.

Ray Hurley, an old friend of Richard's, would be rowing the second boat. The breeze was already fitful at quarter-past eight in the morning, and it would quickly stiffen so that even an average caster would have some difficulty with it. Doug and Ernie combined might have had as much talent as one average caster, or yet again they may not have. They had memorized the insects in the Yellowstone drainage and had flies to match them down to near-pornographic detail, but they didn't have the skills to get these flies out of the boat.

They didn't see it this way. Western fly fishing frequently involves casting tight loops close to the water, at moderate distance, but slapping the fly in hard. Ernie and Doug were from Pennsylvania, and rarely fished water more than a couple rod-lengths wide. Fly fishing was supposed to be slow and graceful. Slow and graceful casting looks nice in the movies and perhaps on a slow eastern creek where the wind never blows, but on the Yellowstone, slow and graceful casting into a fast and graceless wind leads to the fast and graceless formation of a puddle of line around the caster and/or boatman's body.

It didn't help that the fishing was slow.

By lunchtime both Ernie and Doug were fed up. They both thought they needed to be fishing flies that closely matched the (mixed and sparse) hatches on the water, and they both were of the opinion that it was just too windy to fish.

They said as much over sandwiches, bewailing the poor fishing they had. Montana was supposed to be the Promised Land, and this wasn't it.

Ray had listened to Doug's whining all morning, and now had to listen to Ernie's as well. While the fishing wasn't great, both Ray and Richard were skilled enough anglers to know that there were in fact fish to be caught. In those days Richard was able to take a more philosophical standpoint under such conditions: he did his part, putting the boat where it needed to be and giving Ernie the appropriate flies. He even tried to get him to keep his elbow almost motionless, to put a lot of pop in his backcast, to pause long enough to let this backcast straighten to put the energy back into the rod to power the forward cast, and to use a sharp finish on the forward cast to turn the cast over tight and low, thereby putting the Trude six inches from the bank at the base of the willows, where it belonged. If Ernie didn't want to listen, so be it.

Richard fishes primarily for small fish in pocket water with dry flies. It's just what he likes to do. He'd rather catch a nine-inch brookie on a dry than a twenty-inch brown on a nymph. Since nine-inch brookies are rather easier to come by than twenty-inch browns, this has led to him developing a rather casual, non-predatory attitude towards fishing. If his client can't catch anything and complains about it, well, that's all right. There's always the hope that tomorrow's client will be better.

Ray, on the other hand, was a predator. He routinely fished a nine-weight on the Yellowstone, throwing flies better suited to largemouth bass or perhaps pike. He didn't catch as many fish as Richard, but most of his could have eaten several of Richard's fish and still have room to eat a size-1 Whitlock Sculpin.

All morning Ray's drill sergeant streak had slowly but surely been emerging. "You should cast downstream forty-five degrees" had become "Cast downstream forty-five degrees." Then, "Downstream! Forty-five degrees!" Listening to Ernie and Doug complain at lunch brought his anger out still further. They complained about the lack of insects on the water, the flies that matched nothing, and of course the wind. At last Ernie made the definitive statement. "It is simply impossible to cast into this wind."

At this, Ray snapped. "Oh yeah?" he shouted, and grabbed Doug's rod without asking. He stomped down to the river, waded out to his knees, turned downstream, and after two tight, sharp false casts and a short double hall, shot seventy feet of line directly into the teeth of the wind. Then he reeled in, stomped back to the lunch table, tossed down Doug's rod, and turned to the astonished anglers. "Now how's that for impossible!"

They made no reply for some time.

"What's the scientific name of that small, speckle-winged caddis that we're seeing a few of?" Ernie said at last. "I think I'm going to put on an appropriate imitation."

Richard, not to be outdone by Ray's exhibition, and having repeatedly stated all morning that the only fish likely to prefer a precise imitation were whitefish, since there were only a handful of caddis on the water and nothing rising to them, thought back to his college Latin. "That caddis is an *Aurigae trudii*," he replied at last.

"I've never heard of that one," Ernie said.

"It's a #12 Coachman Trude, and it needs to be a foot off the bank."

So that's how the boat they were floating in that day got its name. The replacement for it, after the old boat was battered into an unseaworthy hulk, took the same name, as befits a retired ship that has served honorably and accrued some renown. The next boat, a smaller, low-profile drifter more suited to flatter water and smaller clients, took the other obvious name, *Regis lupii*, Royal Wulff. The replacement for that old boat is currently nameless, since Richard has yet to figure out how to Latinize the phrase "Parachute Adams," but he's working on it.

Litter

In late August 2005, I was on upper Soda Butte trying to get away from people and to catch fish on dries, and was succeeding admirably at the latter goal and mostly at the former. The fish here run smaller than those in the famous water downstream, though an occasional big one will surprise you. I wasn't here for big fish, though. In probably a hundred days of fishing and guiding upstream of Round Prairie, my clients and I have combined for maybe fifty trout over fifteen inches, plus a few more hooked and lost. I was on upper Soda Butte because the lower creek was packed solid with people and on the upper stretch I could find some open water if I walked. The trout were looking up for Green Drakes, which weren't hatching consistently this late in the summer in the warmer water downstream. For a working fishing guide without as much free time as I would like when the fishing is good, the fact that this stretch of the creek is just out of sight of the road but stays almost empty can be a real benefit.

But I wasn't entirely able to get away from the influence of people. Once in a while the roar of a truck with too big an engine penetrated the chuckling of the stream and the brushing of the wind through the trees, and in some muddy spots there were a few telltale flat tracks left by felt-soled wading boots, but these were minor concerns. The thing that wasn't a minor concern was the crushed Budweiser can I found in the middle of a gravel bar on the inside of one of the great bend pools that distinguish upper Soda Butte. The can was unfaded, and not in a place where the current could have deposited it, which meant that someone—probably one of the anglers who had also left boot tracks in the mud—had tossed the can aside, perhaps having cracked it in the first place to celebrate one of the occasional sixteen- or seventeen-inch fish that burst out of the riffle corners to attack a Green Drake once in a blue moon, even up this high on the creek.

•

I find litter everywhere in the Yellowstone drainage, some pieces more obvious than others, but just as pervasive. A lot of it is surely tossed aside by normal tourists, like the cigarette butts and empty soda bottles at the popular pullouts where animals are commonly visible or in the parking lots at the largest attractions, but too much of it is along streams, even in the backcountry.

The most obvious pieces of trash we fly-rodders leave behind are the snarls of leader material that gather in snags. Some of these I can understand: when a current is running hard and chest-deep, there's not much one can do when a leader knot breaks, leaving four or five feet of leader and tippet snarled in a logjam. But some of these tangles are unexplainable. Why would anyone leave a strand of leader hanging from a tree within arm's reach? I'm a short guy, and I retrieve a lot of tangles of leader and tippet material that are easy to grab. This makes me think the answer is probably simple carelessness.

The same goes for flies. Most traditional flies don't matter much as litter, since a bronzed hook will eventually rust away and a fly made from chicken feathers, muskrat fur, and thread will break down under UV light and the action of wind and water. With modern materials, lost or dropped flies become a bigger problem. I've discovered a half-dozen or so enormous foam crickets littering the banks of the Lamar and Soda Butte, bugs with four or five layers of foam that make them as thick around as my thumb, and about as big, probably a #2 or #4 long-shank hook. The hooks on these things will probably rust away with a few rainstorms, but foam in a fly is really no different than foam in a coffee cup, and it will be around long after we're gone, and perhaps after all the trout are gone, too.

I shouldn't talk, of course, since I fish foam myself, if I must, but I try harder not to lose foam flies than I do flies that will break down, and always fish heavy tippets to avoid the snapped backcasts that I believe seal the fate of many of the giant foam crickets. Some people insist on fishing 5X tippet all the time, which is prone to popping on a backcast with poor timing, therefore leaving many large flies hidden in the grass or waiting to snag an elk's foot when it walks across a gravel bar.

The fact that I'll fish foam, and indeed have designed many foam patterns that are sold in Parks' Fly Shop and elsewhere, is a telling one. I like natural materials more, but I'll still use foam when that's what the fish want. "What the fish want" reduces to "What I want," since the ultimate purpose of tying anything on the end of my line is to catch fish, which is something I do for fun. I don't fish with casting gear anymore, and I would probably attack someone I saw slinging an illegal nightcrawler in Yellowstone Park, but someone using a spinning rod and spoon or drifting a worm beneath an undercut has the same ultimate goal that I do, a goal that overrides or at least complicates many other considerations. I know that the foam grasshoppers and beetles I use might wind up crunched into a gravel bar, never to be seen again, foam perhaps a bit tattered but not broken-down, but I still carry boxes of foam hoppers, beetles, and ants.

So do I have any right to complain when I pick up an empty beer can? At least a beer can is something that any passing angler can see, meaning it's likely to get picked up. Most flies vanish into the grass or get hidden beneath rocks. I don't know the answer to this question. Most people, even those who don't fish, probably wouldn't think of a lost or abandoned fly as being in the same league as an abandoned beer can, perhaps because flies are lost in action, if you will, and losing one is usually an accident. Also, a lost fly picked up from a gravel bar tends to be more picturesque than a shiny metal can retrieved from the same gravel bar, and if the fly is in good enough shape, it is still useful, while I doubt anyone with enough money to afford to fly fish would be so hard up as to trade in recyclables for a few cents.

Of course, flies and beer cans are only the most obvious pieces of litter in Yellowstone. Most of the litter in Yellowstone isn't even thought of as such, or is invisible. Soda Butte above Round Prairie is heavily contaminated with mine waste from the inactive gold mines in the creek's headwaters, outside the Park. Some sections have so much cyanide, arsenic, and heavy metal contamination that they are next to lifeless. This problem could get much worse, if the various dams and berms containing the remainder of the mine waste were to fail, during the height of runoff compounded by a thunderstorm, for example. Fishermen were not responsible for this damage, but the difficulty in raising public awareness of the problem suggests that many of the anglers who come to Soda Butte simply don't care, so long as the fish in the lower creek remain large and keep rising.

A form of litter even less visible than the mine waste is definitely something to which anglers contribute. Every second, a fine dust of particulates falls on Soda Butte, and upon every other watershed in Yellowstone, caused by the automobiles virtually every angler uses to get to the water and by the factories that produce the technologically-advanced rods, clothing, and accessories that every fly angler uses. The verdict is still out whether any of this effects Yellowstone Park streams in an appreciable, direct way, considering that Yellowstone certainly has cleaner air than that of, say, Detroit, but the other effects of modern industry are certainly having an appreciable indirect effect. Global warming means less snow in the winter, which in turn means less and warmer water in the creeks in the summer, which in turn means stressed fish and fewer of them. This in turn means unhappy fishermen standing in Soda Butte Creek. Many fly fishers (myself included) consider themselves environmentalists, and many who don't still participate in stream cleanups, donate money to Trout Unlimited or The Federation of Fly Fishers, or at the very least pause to pick up beer cans they find along a creek, but even when we're part of the solution, we're also part of the problem. The real question is whether the good we do outweighs the bad.

•

There's another form of litter that fills the streams and lakes of the Yellowstone region, and it's one for which fishermen are fully to blame, and one that most of us don't feel at all guilty about. I'm talking about the fish.

Consider the cutt-bows I catch in many rivers and creeks in the Yellowstone area. They're beautiful fish, no question about it, arguably more beautiful than either a pure cutthroat or a pure rainbow, especially when the unpredictability of a cross between a fish that has, say, 68% cutthroat genes and one that's 59% rainbow manifests itself in surprising ways in their offspring. They also fight harder than a cutthroat and tend to grow larger than the average local rainbows. Yet they shouldn't be in Bear Creek, or the Yellowstone, or the lower Gardner, or Slough, or the Lamar, or lower Soda Butte, all places where rainbows originally stocked to improve the fishery have hybridized with cutthroats for generation upon generation. Virtually all cutt-bows can spawn successfully, either with rainbows, cutts, or other hybrids, so it's almost impossible to determine if a given fish is actually a real cutthroat or not. Downstream of the Yellowstone Park boundary, introduced rainbows have entirely eliminated 100% pure westslope cutthroats (a different subspecies than the Yellowstone cutthroat found elsewhere in the Park) from the Gallatin drainage. Nowadays many westslope reintroduction efforts are underway, particularly inside the park, but trying to fix old mistakes doesn't really absolve us of making these mistakes in the first place.

Or consider the Gardner River drainage. There were no fish above Osprey Falls historically, since the native cutts and Rocky Mountain Whitefish were unable to climb the plunge. Early in the 20th century, brook trout and rainbows were stocked above the falls, altering a unique ecosystem: a healthy, relatively productive watershed with climax species other than fish. Below Osprey Falls a few cutts still swim, but they are few and far between. Now rainbows and browns predominate. Some people even regard these non-natives as more worthwhile a trout than the native cutthroats—the only native trout species in the Park. The fall run of browns into the Gardner, when fish from as far away as forty miles down the Yellowstone ascend almost to Osprey Falls to spawn, is more highly-regarded than the early season fishing for resident trout, and many anglers wish the Park Service would keep stocking nonnatives.

The word "litter" may be a bit too gentle a term for some of these introductions. "Systematic pollution" might be more accurate.

Of course, humans have been bringing new species into Yellowstone for over a century, if not for the millennia since the glaciers receded, and elsewhere in the world this process has continued at least since the advent of agriculture. Some of these species have made themselves at home without definitively harming the ecosystems into which they were placed. The mountain goats that occasionally look down at anglers on Soda Butte from the crags of Baronette Peak are nonnative, but they didn't replace any other large herbivores. Others, like the lake trout in Yellowstone Lake and the New Zealand mud snails in some of Yellowstone's rivers—both species introduced by anglers, purposefully in the first case and accidentally in the latter—have seriously damaged the ecosystems into which they were placed. Similar contradictory results have occurred throughout the world. Few would consider the introduction of honeybees or horses into the New World disasters (though they may have replaced native species), while the introduction of starlings into Central Park ranks as one of the great "What were you thinking?" moments in American history.

The above are only introductions of animals: if plants are considered, still more human alterations become apparent. Even as I write this, spotted knapweed spores picked off an angler's tackle and dropped along the banks of Soda Butte or the Gardner last summer are waiting for spring, ready to begin their work of choking native grasses. While some human introductions are purposeful efforts either by government officials or individuals to change the natural landscape (nonnative trout) and some are incidental (snails or even the quiet patter of particulates falling into a creek), the introduction of knapweed into the region is a result of being careless with what we toss aside, "littering" in the same sense that throwing aside a beer can is littering.

But I pick up beer cans whenever I find them alongside a stream, while not thinking twice about fishing for browns in the Gardner. In fact, I'm happier when I get a nice runner brown than when I get a cutthroat out of that stream, since I can go somewhere on the Yellowstone or in the Lamar drainage when I'm in the mood to catch cutts. It all comes back to the fact that I'm a fisherman, one who likes to catch a variety of species using a variety of techniques. If I was given a time machine to go back and stop Captain Boutelle from stocking brook trout in the upper Gardner, I would certainly do it. If I could keep lake trout out of Yellowstone Lake and New Zealand mud snails from infesting the Park, I would. If I could keep the mines from impacting Soda Butte, making it less likely that one day I'll go fish upper Soda Butte for the first time some season and find it fishless from a cyanide release, I would certainly do that too. Yet I'd stock the upper Gardner with cutthroats out of Slough Creek without a second thought, and the other actions would spring as much from my desire to fish Yellowstone until the day I die as an altruistic desire to preserve ecosystems in their natural state.

So I deplore some actions examples of "littering," yet I don't worry about others. Does this make me a hypocrite? Maybe it does. It certainly makes me a fisherman.

Creep Days

When I took my lunch break today, about a fifth of the flecks of drizzle that struck me while I stood outside the local burger stand waiting for my food were actually snowflakes. They melted as soon as they struck me, but they were there nonetheless, the first snowflakes of the season. Someone mentioned that West Yellowstone was supposed to get ten inches of snow tonight, and the weather radio mentioned the noon observations from Yellowstone Lake and Old Faithful—31 degrees and snowing and 32 degrees and snowing, respectively. It is the 16th of September.

If I were still in Washington, days like today would bring thoughts of steelhead as though they gusted in on the cold north wind. I'd want to be butt-deep in the Skykomish or Stillaguamish, swinging something purple and black and hideous, like an Egg-Sucking Leech with silver dumbbell eyes tied on a 6X-long streamer hook with the point clipped off and a little, wide-gape stinger hook hanging off the back, hiding in the tail. I have taken the majority of my late summer-run steelhead on such rigs in the fall, even though they're usually thought of as more-suited to winter steelhead. Here in Montana such flies would only terrify the fish, but similarly-ugly nymphs work great. Instead of an Egg-Sucking Leech day, it's a Creep Day.

A Creep is fly that looks like it can't work, except maybe for bluegill or, indeed, enraged steelhead. The pattern has a body of flash chenille, the rear half black and the front orange, a copper bead or conehead, and six or eight white rubber legs depending on size. All this is tied on a 3X-long hook, usually a streamer hook or a natural bend hook, between size-2 and size-8. I usually weight mine with .035 gauge tin wire and a tungsten bead or cone, and always fish them on a seven-weight. A pile of them on my tying desk always brings a laugh from customers in the store. Even when I say I fish the flies, the sparkle in their eyes suggests that most think I'm full of it.

Of course, I usually tie an entire season's worth of Creeps in mid-August, when for most people thoughts of hideous nymphs with rubber legs poking in all directions are anathema. By mid-September these flies are safe and secure in my fall-run brown trout box. Under gray dismal skies, when customers pull off gloves upon walking in the store, the pattern seems to make a lot more sense. Of course, when the browns are in and aggressive, I don't necessarily want anyone else to know about it, unless they're my clients for the next day.

This season I got to the Creeps late. Only a frantic call from my dad got me going on them. It gets gray and dismal in September in Missouri too, though not so gray and dismal as it is here today, and he'd had an excellent day a few days before, bumping a Creep through the riffles at Bennett Spring. His last Creep was falling apart, and he was desperate for more.

Runner browns are known to go for this sort of thing, especially late in the spawning season or during cold snaps early, when the rivers get cold and the skies darken enough for the fish to feel secure. This is why I always carry a few when I'm chasing runners. Yet the pattern has a dirty little secret: the rainbows actually like it as much as the browns.

My dad had tied on a Creep hoping for a brown, but what he got was twenty or thirty rainbows. I like the pattern the most in late September, during the brief lull between the early run of browns and the main push. With water temperatures dropping, the rainbows are hungry, and with gray skies common and the light flat for longer periods even when we have a late September bluebird day, the Creep gets the larger rainbows interested more successfully than a Blue-winged Olive or a smaller nymph. If a brown takes it, so much the better.

•

I mostly use the Creep on the Gardner, twitching it through riffles swarming with fish rising to Blue-winged Olives, fish that eat the Creep just as readily. On other rivers, Creep Days might be better called Something Else Days, but I still call them Creep Days. Creep Days are weird days.

The Grand Canyon of the Yellowstone is primarily dry fly and nymph water, but in the fall I sometimes have days where what the fish want is a #4

Muddler or something even more unusual. In the fall of 2003 I had been having trouble getting good drifts during a BWO hatch, since I'd given my dad the better spot to fish to a pod of risers, and out of frustration I tied on an enormous Zoo Cougar I'd tied for an upcoming trip to British Columbia. The big, yellow and white pseudo-sculpin didn't sink until I'd made a half-dozen casts, but in those six casts I had two fish rise from the deeps to smash the enormous fly as it skated across the surface like a mouse pattern in Alaska. I missed both fish out of shock, but the third, a nine-incher, I hooked squarely and landed. The fly was half as long as the fish. Over the next twenty minutes I caught another four fish, until the curious frenzy stopped as suddenly as it had begun. Some might say that the fish attacked the fly because they were cutthroats, and therefore stupid, but this cannot explain the last fish I caught on the fly, a sixteen-inch rainbow that gave off eating Blue-wings to eat the Zoo Cougar. That was a great Creep Day.

More commonly, Creep Days on the Gardner are conventional streamer days elsewhere. Most of my sixty- or seventy-fish days on the Yellowstone have come on brooding, gray afternoons in the fall, when the Turck's Tarantula and Four Feather nymph combo brought nothing, the Trude didn't work, the Blue-wings didn't emerge, and even Matt's Stoneflies drifted through the deep slots brought only a few little fish. Yet as soon as I tied on a PT-Bugger, I had multiple fish racing each other for the chance to eat it. I even caught an eight-inch brookie who'd come down from Tower or Antelope Creek to risk the big river and its hungry cutts, rainbows, and hybrids.

Some days it's another bug, even a dry. In fact, about the only thing Creep Days have in common is the weather: it's always about six inches this side of nasty. On one such day while floating the Yellowstone between Corwin Springs and the head of Yankee Jim, all my clients were catching during the Blue-winged Olive hatch were whitefish gathered in the riffles to spawn. The day before, my dad and I had floated the same stretch and had brought plenty of cutts and rainbows to the net. We hadn't seen any really big fish, but there had been a few fifteen- or sixteen-inchers, and I had expected more of the same on the day I was getting paid. Thus I was thrown for a loop by the poor fishing. By eleven o'clock, each of my sports had landed at least a dozen whitefish apiece, and three trout between them. Nowhere near enough. That's when I had them start fishing Trudes on the swing, and when they started catching fish. A lot of them. Twenty or more apiece over the rest of the day, and lots more hooked and lost.

The rainbows and cutts were hanging further down the riffles than the whitefish, and they were in a mood to chase things. Perhaps they were taking emerging Blue-winged Olives, or perhaps they would have eaten small streamers just as well as the Trude. I should have made one of my clients try swinging a Muddler just under the surface, perhaps on a riffle hitch as though we were looking for steelhead.

The trout that feed so voraciously on unusual things on Creep Days actually call steelhead to mind. There are large differences, of course: steelhead don't eat for food but out of aggression, there are fewer of them, and they're much larger. Yet both the trout that suddenly become aggressive and the steelhead that leave off eating Spades and other small, unobtrusive low water patterns in favor of Big Uglies as soon as the weather turns bad are responding to the gray weather and the change in water temperatures. Both now have a greater sense of urgency. For steelhead the spawning season is imminent, for resident trout it is the looming cold of winter, when there will be limited food available and the trout will lack the energy to pursue what food there is. Both steelhead and residents know they must prepare. The steelhead gather themselves to fight for mates or for the prime gravel in which to dig their nests, the rainbows gather themselves to survive the lean season ahead.

Perhaps the way I respond to the change of seasons is not so different from the fish I pursue. The steelhead begin to prefer a gaudy bulky pattern, the trout turn away from delicate insects on the surface and aggressively chase large nymphs instead, and I begin to prefer gaudy, bulky, colored-up steelhead and big, pretty brown trout.

Rafting Johnson's Shut-Ins, Sort of

I was seventeen. This probably explains why I decided to run a rubber boat through Johnson's Shut-Ins as a break from a fishing trip with my cousin Jack. He had done it during the high water of mid-May, and now, in midsummer, there would be more girls to impress, which had been Jack's goal and would be mine, as well. Any extra shots of adrenaline in my system would be a bonus. We'd fish in the morning, and, if all went well, by noon I'd have bikini-clad beauties hanging on either arm, impressed at my willingness to risk life and limb in a more creative way than merely throwing myself off a cliff into the river, the way most guys showed off for the girls.

 Some explanation is probably in order. Johnson Shut-Ins is a place in southeast Missouri where the

East Fork of the Black River cuts down through a lava rock canyon. The river splits into a many as twenty or thirty narrow, deep channels here that split and twine like webs through the rocks. Time and water have combined to create weird spires of black rock sticking up out of the water, strange circular basins carved by eddying sand, and, most importantly, innumerable cascades, slides, and secluded pools. In many ways it is similar to the Tiemann Shut-Ins at Millstream Gardens Conservation area on the St. Francis River, which I discuss in a different story in this collection, but Johnson Shut-Ins is a gentler, more playful place. The current is less intense, the trails along the stream are better, and there are more chutes and slides. In other words, Johnson Shut-Ins is a natural water park, particularly for teenagers who have enough money for gas but not enough to pay for a real life actual water park.

I have no recollection of how the fishing went. We probably caught enough fish, since we were still fishing at 9:30 when the first sunbathers, swimmers, and rock-scramblers interrupted our angling. By 10:00 several gaggles of teenage girls began to arrive, to apply suntan lotion, to frolic, to giggle, to glance flirtatiously, and to otherwise contrive to make my backcast fall apart. I turned to Jack and said, "It's time." We reeled in and quick-marched back to the car.

More groups of teens as well as families passed us as we pumped up my raft in the day-use parking lot. They all gawked. Clearly an eight-foot bright yellow raft from K-Mart was not something they considered appropriate. We scowled at the families and smiled at the girls. I would show all of them.

The Taum Sauk Trail crosses the river on a footbridge maybe a half-mile above the shut-ins. That's where we decided to put in, so I could get a feel for how the boat handled and so my cousin to get a few casts in from a boat. I didn't realize it at the time, but this was my first experience rowing a boat on flowing water while somebody fished. Thank the Trout Gods I've gotten a lot better at it.

The first couple hundred yards went fine. The river was deep in most places, and even the shallow spots were riffles with well-rounded stones along their bottoms, so when we did drag all was well. Still, I got to thinking that the river was a lot lower now, in July, than it usually is in May, when Jack had done his float. When we dragged through the last riffle before big, volcanic boulders began to predominate, still a couple hundred yards above the shut-ins, I started to think I might have a bit of trouble reaching the Cliff Pool, the big pool that marked the end of the shut-in, a couple hundred yards downstream of the steepest, most tangled section.

I made Jack bail out when we started bumping boulders. He'd walk the rest of the way to the top of the chutes, then slip/slide/swim as usual down to what we called the Middle Pool, below the most heavily-braided section of the river, before rejoining me for the last run down to the Cliff Pool. The boat handled better without his weight, but quick handling didn't prevent me from running over a sharp lava rock before I even reached the Upper Pool, just above the steep section. A stream of bubbles erupted beside the boat as one of my two floor chambers was torn open. The hull was still sound, however, so after getting out to check the boat I hopped back in. Onward!

I reached the top of the chutes without further incident, eyed all the way by perplexed families playing in the relatively calm waters upstream of the section that resembles a waterpark. Then, as per Jack's suggestions, I shipped my oars and leaned forward onto my knees, to guide the boat through the narrow twisty channels by hand paddling and pushing off the rock walls. Then I was into the first drop. The front of the boat fell away, followed by the stern, and I began to pick up speed...

...and came to a halt between two pillars of rock. The current pushed feebly at the back of the boat, unable to push it through the gap. As irritated teens climbed around me while I clambered out of the boat to get it unstuck, I reflected again that the flows of midsummer are not as high as those of spring.

Eventually I got the boat moving again, and for a time all was well. I slid down two chutes without incident, then came to another. I struck this one at a weird angle, so that at the bottom the boat flipped forward, with me leading the way. On my knees, with hands outstretched to paddle, I could do nothing to keep myself in the boat, and fell forward out of it, hands grasping wildly to no avail for anything to stop my fall. A rock rushed up towards me, but, miraculously, my face hit the water six inches to its right. The adrenaline rush from that was a bit much.

In the interim, my boat had struck another sharp rock, or perhaps it was simply moving fast enough that abrading against one of the volcanic pillars was enough to put pinholes in one of the main chambers. My brave yellow craft was going limp.

My cousin had used his boat for hours and had not popped it. Again I was reminded that July is not May.

The girls I passed, or that passed me as I pulled my way through the tight spots since the current was too feeble to do it, looked either annoyed or amused. I could have accepted the popped boat, since I never used it anyway, but annoyed girls and girls laughing at me were not things I had bargained for.

Still, I had a few more chutes and one good plunge before the Middle Pool, so there was nothing to do but continue on. I dropped another pair of rapids without incident, then tried to squeeze through too-narrow a chute and popped my raft's second main chamber. The top of the raft was starting to pancake.

I had to rock back and forth to get over the five-foot plunge at the bottom of this chute, the tallest sheer drop in the shut-in, the one I'd been looking forward to since hatching my plan to float Johnson's Shut-Ins in the first place.

At least I'd been looking forward to it until I almost landed on somebody, a man in his late twenties or thirties, who shouted curses at me as I paddled past. That reaction was closer to what I was looking for. Anger from some old guy wasn't as nice as adoration from lovely ladies, but it wasn't bad. My boat, however, was now in terrible shape. In barely missing the guy, I landed on a sharp rock that popped my last remaining intact air chamber, which meant the boat was starting to sink under my weight when I at last paddled into the Middle Pool. Though Jack rushed towards me, to continue the float as planned, I bailed over the side and opened the main valves, releasing two measly puffs of air and putting my boat out of its misery. If I was going to get an adrenaline rush or meet any young ladies, I'd have to do these things in the usual way.

Unfortunately, the girls had seen my attempt to navigate the canyon. Not a one paid any attention to my aerial moves off the cliffs, even when I did a flip off one of the lower rocks. I was frustrated, but in the end things worked out, because ever since I've been a lot more serious about my fishing.

The Other Side of the River

Cars and trucks slowed down when they saw me. By now, I was used to it. I was standing on a narrow shelf of rock knee-deep in the Gardner River, back against a vertical rock face on the far side of the river from the road, catching fish on what seemed like every cast. The Gardner can be like that during the Salmonfly hatch, though most of my fish were eating the caddis I was fishing behind the stonefly. In the moments between fish, I would look up and see the gawkers staring. They were certainly interested in the fish, since when you think about it, seeing someone hook, play, or land a fish while driving past is pretty difficult, since for somebody in a car an angler on foot is only in sight for thirty seconds, if that.

They also had to be wondering how in the hell I managed to get where I was. The nearest bridge was a quarter-mile upstream and separated from the stretch I was fishing by an impassable stretch of whitewater with a sheer rock face on my side, making downstream travel from the bridge impossible, and there was a similar obstruction not far downstream of me on my side. Moreover, this entire stretch of the Gardiner is a chute of class-III whitewater, in mid-July still waist-deep in most places.

I'll say two things about how I got across. One, there's this one particular spot where a crazy wet wader can make it. Two, I am careful, and don't carry anything I don't mind getting wet. So far as I know, this spot is the only one where it's possible to wade across the Gardner until August this far down, only two miles from the Yellowstone confluence and in a steep, narrow canyon. Since I usually don't like to walk all the way back to the ford when I'm done fishing, I usually wind up just half-swimming back to the road side when I'm done. In the middle of summer it's refreshing, and only a bit terrifying due to the whitewater.

Despite the difficulty of the crossing and the necessity of swimming at the end of the day, getting to the opposite side of the river here is almost always worth it. Though it'll never be a Madison or Henry's Fork because it has so few dense hatches and so few large resident fish (most resident fish here run eight to twelve inches), the Gardner does flow right alongside the road over much of its length and is known to every fly shop in a hundred-mile radius as a good bet during Salmonfly season and at any time for an average angler who isn't afraid of fast water, so it does get fished some. Because the middle of the river is still a raging torrent in July, impossible to cast across and still get a decent drift, wading the river allows me to target fish that have seen few flies. Once I fished this stretch of river with my dad, who isn't as strong a wader as I. The Salmonfly hatch was in full swing, and I probably caught sixty fish in four hours, fishing on the side opposite the road. My dad, on the road side, got five.

•

That stretch of the Gardner is an odd case. Most of the time, streams that flow alongside the road are easily wadable, or they have enough bridges that an angler willing to walk two or three hundred yards upstream or down from one of the crossings can cover both sides while barely getting his or her feet wet. Still, the side opposite the road frequently doesn't get fished all that much, especially on pocket water creeks. It's as if anglers don't trust their eyes: the fast, whitewater creek must be uncrossable, even where it sure *looks* like it's less than knee deep. I don't know how many times I've been asked how I got to my side of a creek when there's an easy ford a hundred yards upstream.

Of course, sometimes people willfully choose to ignore these fords. Soda Butte Creek, which flows less than a mile from the road throughout its length and loops back on itself in curves a snake would envy, is one such place. Though one must be willing to put up with crowds on popular streams like this, the lack of manners some other anglers display can make me want to give up fishing frontcountry streams with big trout. Almost. I remember one day when I was fishing towards a juicy, undercut bank on the road side, at the head of an old, firmly-established pool called Beaver Hole by some locals. The fish were rising rather fussily to a sparse Pale Morning Dun hatch, and the best fish were all within a foot of the undercut. Perhaps to look into the deep, mysterious depths along this undercut, years of tourist anglers had beaten a path no more than two feet back from the bank, along the top of the undercut.

I know tourists had beaten the track because any local—or any native of the Rockies or anywhere else wild, spooky trout can be found, for that matter— knows that you *never* walk along a high bank if you can help it. On this stretch of creek there are good fords at every riffle corner, including one twenty yards upstream of where I was fishing, so that by the time Soda Butte becomes fishable you can *always* help it.

This fact didn't stop a party of four guys (two too many to be fishing together on Soda Butte) from tromping downstream past the good ford and right along the top of the beautiful undercut I was casting towards. I knew what was going to happen, but despite the sinking feeling in my gut I called out, "Would you guys mind stepping fifteen or twenty feet from the bank? I'm fishing to some risers right under the bank, and the trail is close enough that you'll spook them."

The apparent leader of the group, resplendent in brand-new waders, snazzy chest pack and lanyard, up-downer hat, and painfully-pink caped angling shirt, paused and squinted across the creek at me. I was wet-wading in wading shoes and neoprene booties on their last legs, threadbare jean shorts, and a vest that had seen five hundred days on the river without a washing. By his expression, I did not quite measure up. "The trail's right here," he said, as though staying on the trail was some law of nature.

"And it's too close," I replied. "The fish can see you when you walk along the trail."

"We're far enough back," he said, and resumed walking. The fish stopped rising for ten minutes, of course.

At times, fishing on the other side of the river from the road can bring a twisted sort of solitude. While traffic rushes by sixty or seventy feet away and motorcyclists drop to idle for a moment to watch as they cruise by, you can fish water that no one else has thought to visit. Yet this pseudo-solitude brings pseudo-invisibility. On Soda Butte, which is certainly small enough everywhere to fish the entire width of the stream from either side, I've had anglers casually walk up the road side, fishing the same pool I was already on, until they'd gone right past me, spooking every fish in sight. These days I wouldn't stand for such an intrusion, since I became something of an early-onset curmudgeon in my mid-twenties, but during my first couple seasons in Yellowstone I was still unsure of myself, and let it happen with some regularity.

The best other sides of the river are always in places where it looks impossible to get across. The other side of the Yellowstone just below Tower Creek is like this. Not only is this stretch of river invisible from a casual angler's lookout just above the mouth of the creek at river level, but the canyon itself is deep enough that someone in a car creeping along the face of the canyon wall could not hope to see it. A trail does drop in to the far side of the river through a notch in the ridge above, but it's a narrow, twisty little track kept maintained only by the steps of extremely surefooted anglers and elk, which deters many anglers and convinces many others to drop in a quarter-mile upstream of a point opposite the creek mouth. The Yellowstone where the trail drops in is funneled into a tight little gorge, and in July and August, when *both* sides of the river can at times get too crowded for my taste, there isn't even a place slow and shallow enough to *fish* more than a few feet out from the bank for a half-mile upstream. Downstream the canyon walls close in even more, and there are boulder fields on both sides that have never felt the step of man. I'm willing to swim three or four strokes to fish the other side of the Gardner, but on this stretch of the Yellowstone it'd be more like fifty strokes, with spin cycle whitewater downstream and three-foot breakers even in the calm spots. I don't know anybody who's tried it, and never will myself.

Yet in some years, sometimes as early as early September, sometimes as late as a week before the end of the season, the one wide spot in the entire two-mile stretch of water made accessible by the Tower Falls trail becomes shallow enough for an intrepid wader who knows the route to get across. There's still spin cycle whitewater close enough downstream that a spill could mean a long-term stay in the river, but by wading across at a slight upstream angle from some islands, it is possible to stay no more than waist deep all the way across, provided the gravel doesn't wash out from under your feet. Where the ford gets to the other side there isn't much good water for a long way in either direction. An angler who crosses above the islands must walk back downstream once they're across to find good water. In other words, they've got to know the river to know that the tough crossing is worth it.

The first time I made the trip was, as is often the case with such endeavors, the best. I'd fished the Tower side for an hour or so, hoping that the Blue-winged Olives that had hatched in dense clouds during a September snow storm would be back (it was now early October), or at least that the fish in the good run below the mouth of the creek would be interested in my PT-Bugger. I caught a few on the streamer, but I discovered to my disappointment that the good run below the creek where the trout had been rising so well a couple weeks earlier was no longer a run at all: the river had dropped so much that it was only knee-deep, and also slow. This late in the year, with the river running so clear that I could see fish finning at the bottom of eight-foot deep holes, there were no fish in this water.

The few cutts I did catch were in one of the deep holes, and had taken the streamer fished on a dead drift under a sink-tip with two of my largest tin shot pinched on for even more weight—not exactly exciting fishing. I looked longingly at the run across the river and a bit downstream, a run lined with enormous boulders and swirling with odd currents that I was sure must have deposited sudden shelves of sand and gravel and dug out bottomless holes that would be filled with cutts, and decided to wade up to the islands and go for it.

I was surprised at how easy the crossing was, though in hindsight a lot of that was due to the past summer spent wading aggressively in mountain streams and rivers when it was warm enough that a dunking wouldn't be so bad. After close to five months of fishing or guiding about six days a week, I was in peak form. So I breasted the river with little difficulty and made my way down to the boulder field that had looked so luscious from the road side. I fished a little on the way and caught two or three fish, on the PT-Bugger, but there were really only two spots to target on the entire walk, both marginal.

I made up for it in the boulder field. It seemed like every twelve- to fourteen-inch cutt in the Yellowstone was stacked in fifty yards of river, most of them packed like sardines into the hole at the edge of the boulder fields, the analogue to the now-vanished run on the other side. This hole was so deep that its depths still shone green-blue, its bottom invisible, despite the glass-clear water. The current ran hard on the outside edge of this hole, and though this late in the year the current seam was straight, with the hard current line and a steady, soft flow over the top of the run each clearly demarcated, earlier in the year there must have been a huge backeddy over the top of the hole, because the shelf of sand interspersed with gravel upon which I stood dropped off into the abyss as though cut by a giant knife. One step it would have been knee-deep on a child, the next it would have floated a giant's hat. I stood atop one of the boulders poking up from the sand, cast my streamer on a short sink-tip to the edge of the fast current, let it sink, then stripped it back with quick, jerky strokes and my rod tip held high. Just before reaching the drop off, I'd quit stripping, toss out a loop of line, and lower my rod tip all the way to the surface. My PT-Bugger would be swimming along at high speed a couple feet under the surface, then suddenly lunge for the depths, as though suddenly noticing a predator trailing it and hoping to reach the murky depths and safety.

Most of the time, a cutt would follow the fly through the hole, three or four feet behind, as though unsure of whether or not they should eat the mottled brown, tan, and gray thing swimming so blithely across the river. When I dropped the rod, they would dart forward and grab it in a mad rush. I have no idea how many fish I caught in an hour or so of doing this, but I do remember my best streak included strikes or fish landed on thirteen consecutive casts. The grass isn't always greener on the other side of the fence, but in this case the fishing was certainly better on the other side of the river.

•

I didn't do quite that good on the Gardner that afternoon, but I did well enough. I even caught a double, with one fish on the Salmonfly and another on the caddis dropper. It took me a couple hours to get to the narrow spot in the canyon where it becomes impossible to get any further upstream on the side opposite the road, longer than usual since I was catching so many fish. Then I was faced either with a long walk downstream to the spot where I crossed in the first place, or a swim. It was getting dark, though it was still warm, and I was worn out, so I took a deep breath and waded to midriver as quickly as I could. When the footing started to go, I pushed off in a lunging half-dive and did a one-armed crawl stroke for three or four strokes, awkwardly kicking with my heavy, wading shoe-clad feet, until I was past the main current tongue and could stand up again, every inch of me dropping. I always tell myself I'm going to turn around when I'm done fishing and walk back down to the ford to keep myself dry from mid-thigh up, but I never do. I know my habits, so I always carry a towel when I fish this stretch of the Gardner, to keep my car from getting too wet.

The few cars that passed as I was breaking down my rod slowed, and one or two even honked. The shadows were getting long and the light flat, so I'm sure at least some of the occupants wondered what I was for a moment before realizing that I was a dripping-wet fisherman and not a bear or sasquatch. Two of the cars did the little double honk that tends to signify amusement, or perhaps sympathy. I was back on the road side, so I imagine most figured that I had taken a bad step and gotten soaked by accident. I doubt any thought I had only minutes before been on the other side of the steep, turbulent river, which in this light looked like a roaring, foamy torrent, impossible for someone to cross, even if he was a sasquatch.

The Ledge Pool

If a prospective angler were to try to find it on a map, there's no way he or she could identify the location of the ledge pool. It seems impossible for it to be where it is. Upstream and down the banks are open and wide, and save for the three- to six-foot-deep trough in which the Gardner River itself flows, the going is flat and easy, amid fragrant sage, grass, and scattered trees. The ledge pool is in a place where a topographic map would suggest the river should be pinched into roaring froth, with high banks making the contour lines stack to either side. Yet instead of flowing swift and white here, it is upstream and down where the river tumbles as pocket water, where mostly small trout live. The pool is long and narrow, with a hard current tongue running down its center but soft water to either side and deep pockets at its head. The top half of the pool, above the old travertine ledge that cuts across the width of the pool at an almost perfect 90-degree angle, is deep enough that even heavy flies fished on long tippets require long casts and perfect drifts to reach bottom, where large fish live. There are whitefish all summer, an occasional big rainbow or hybrid, and in late summer and early fall, the first runner browns up out of the Yellowstone. A lot of them.

The pool is a mile upriver from the nearest trailhead, and off-trail by a couple hundred yards. Upstream, it's a hard half-mile bushwhack to the nearest road, out of sight around several bends and high on a bench, hundreds of vertical feet over the river. Elk descend this bench, but seldom people. For long stretches above and below the ledge pool, the most common fish are small rainbows, fish that must work hard to survive in this fast stretch of stream above Boiling River, in which the water is cold all summer long and not fertile. Above and below the pool, the day's best resident trout might measure thirteen inches, with something truly special going fifteen or sixteen, and most trout are less than ten. Thus this section of river falls under the radar, so that even when the lower Gardner beside the road and the high country sections where brook trout live are crowded, I expect to find the pool empty of anglers, and filled with browns. Each time I come around the last bend and see another person nymphing the long, deep pool, I feel a shock, as though I had never seen another angler before. This has happened only three times.

The ledge pool owns a characteristic no other place can claim; I have been delayed from fishing it more often by animals than anglers. Twice I have seen elk in the woods just downstream of the pool, and had to pause while I waited for them to make way, and once unexpected bighorn sheep filled the hillside to the east. The last time the culprit was a bear, a young black bear attempting to find a territory for itself before it came time to hibernate. I hid in the bushes on the opposite side of the river, downwind and uphill, and the bear passed fifty yards from me, unaware of my presence. I regret that I didn't have a camera that day, my last in Yellowstone Country during the fall of 2004. I was convinced the River Gods would grant me more browns if I did not have a way to record my catch, meaning that anyone who heard the day's tally would think I was making up stories.

I was right on both counts.

•

I don't remember the first time I fished the pool. It might have been the first time I bushwhacked downriver from the road, or it might not have. If it was that day, I would have been fishing dry flies and been mightily unimpressed by the deep, hard-bottomed pool with the sharp current tongue running down its center, as it is too flat and too deep to hold fish willing to come to a dry during the middle of a clear July afternoon.

The first fish I remember coming from the pool was a client's rather than mine. We reached the pool at the end of his morning half-day trip, and though he had never fished with a fly rod before that morning he managed three or four small rainbows and a couple whitefish downstream of the pool. As he could not yet handle slack, I had him fishing flies that could be fished on a slight swing, a Minch's Golden Stone nymph with a Bead, Hare, and Copper on a dropper underneath. I could see several large fish flashing at the bottom of the pool, among the jumbled boulders upstream of the travertine ledge that divides the rainbow water downstream from the brown and whitefish water in its upper half of the pool. I thought they were whitefish, but my client wouldn't mind, and I had him run his nymph down the slot just inside the current tongue down the middle of the pool. On his first cast, he hooked a large fish. It bulldogged along the bottom as whitefish are wont to do, and the silver and white flashes I saw sparking from its sides convinced me that this was what it was. Thus I was surprised when he at last brought the fish to the surface for me to net, and I saw that it was a seventeen-inch rainbow, by far the largest I'd ever seen from this high on the Gardner, to that point in my guiding career.

It was past time to go, he was ecstatic with both the numbers of fish he had landed and the size of this last one, and I always like to quit on a fish—a vicarious fish when I'm guiding. I filed the spot away, but was unable to return that day or that season, since I left for my senior year of college back in the humid Midwest only three days later. The night before I left, I hooked two browns from runs downriver, and landed one. The fish I caught went twenty inches exactly and had shoulders like a spaniel, and it ran me thirty yards downriver before tiring. The second fish, the last I hooked in Yellowstone that season, seemed to hold off running after it felt the sting of the hook, as though it were considering its options. Big fish are known to do that. Then it lunged upstream through forty feet of fast riffle as though my drag did not exist, dove under a rock, and broke me off. This run took perhaps ten seconds. I never saw the fish, but local tier Matt Minch, the originator of the stonefly pattern mentioned above, had hooked a fish he estimated at five pounds in that very spot the previous day, a fish that fought exactly as this one had, which had also broken off. Both the fish I landed and the one Matt and I failed to land would have found their way to the ledge pool, I am certain. Spawning season was a month or more away, and the pool is the first adequate long-term holding water for fish so large for almost a mile.

I am sure fish almost as large already lurked at the bottom of the ledge pool; I have hooked them, though all have escaped.

•

Somehow, I didn't fish the ledge pool my second season in Yellowstone. If memory serves, this was the season I was most preoccupied with small freestone streams where I was sure to fish alone, where I could fish dry flies to eager small brook trout or cutthroats. I don't know if I caught a single runner that season, since I left a week earlier in the year, for my grad school orientation program.

The following year, 2003, I stayed until the last week of the season, the stresses of a graduate program in creative writing in grim northern Missouri—far from any fly fishing whatsoever—having proven too much to bear. Yet again, it was a client who caught the first fish of the season from the ledge pool, and again the client was a rookie. She had landed one or two brook trout earlier in the afternoon, tiny fish from Winter Creek, fish so small they could barely inhale her Trude. I don't know if she had another strike. Until the browns, that is. Pocket water had proven difficult for her, so as a last resort while her husband flogged the water downstream and landed small rainbow after small rainbow, I hurried her far upriver to the ledge pool. Again, I hoped for a whitefish, though I suspected there might be browns present. She hooked but lost a fish almost immediately. It took on her first cast, before she was ready, before she had any control at all over her slack, and shot off upstream towards the head of the pool, cartwheeling across the surface, more out of the water than in. With so much slack and so many aerial maneuvers, it was no surprise when the fish escaped.

The second fish took on her third cast. Despite the adrenaline that I'm sure was coursing through her, she kept undue slack from the line, managed a perfect drift, and flawlessly hooked and fought a brown as energetic as the first. This fish was longer than the bow of my net, seventeen inches or so, and fat. If the many, many fish my clients and I have caught from the pool since this afternoon could be said to fit some sort of template, this fish was the mold.

•

I've caught fish from five spots in the pool. In the tailout, rainbows rise to caddis and Blue-winged Olives at evening. Most of these rainbows are small, but I did get one fourteen-incher once. I typically ignore them. Not once have I caught a runner from this portion of the pool.

Occasionally there will be a runner at the head of the pool, behind the rock that provides just enough of a current break to create a six or seven-foot slick about a foot wide. This is where I caught my first runner last season, a sixteen-incher that ate a black stonefly nymph larger than any of the stoneflies actually present in the river, a #2 fly with a giant hackle and a flashback. The fish took so hard that it almost jerked my rod out of my hand. The third spot is beside this one, three or four feet away, against the opposite bank up under a juniper tree. It's an eddy the size of a bathtub, four or five feet deep. I have only taken one fish from this spot, but I continue to fish it thoroughly, just in case. These two spots are the most dependable runner holding water when the river is still running hard, as it is when the first runners ascend in early August. This early, the other spots are still buried under the hard current tongue running down the middle of the pool, a seam that makes it difficult to get one's flies down until autumn.

Yet it is these two spots along the seam that have produced the greatest number of browns over the years, the places I almost always get at least a strike, if there are any browns in the river yet at all. Both spots aren't really individual pockets at all, but areas about the size of a pool table where the bottom structure and current seams converge to provide excellent overhead cover and slow currents near the bottom. Looking upstream, the first is at the halfway point of the pool, right up against the travertine ledge that bisects the pool. By this point in the pool, the hard current line has spread out and flattened a bit, and by early fall it is slow enough here that the bottom may be seen clearly, without interference from the thousands of shifting prisms formed by the river's broken surface. The fish in this spot hide under the travertine ledge, demanding an odd drift wherein one's fly is downstream of the indicator or the fly line, so that the fly can slip in beneath the ledge unimpeded, rather than being deflected by a tight leader above. This is a dangerous spot to send a fly; I have lost many beneath the ledge.

Hooking a fish here is like alchemy. With the fly floating on a slack line downstream, there are no conscious signs of a strike. Still, perhaps one time in ten when I think I have a strike when drifting my fly beneath the ledge, I do. Even late in the fall, it is most often a whitefish. Because the water surface here is not as broken as it is in the last spot, the best spot in the pool, which a drift must cover to reach the travertine ledge spot in the first place, the browns tend to fill the upper spot first, taking lies beneath the ledge only when first entering the pool or when the spot just upstream already has several fish in it. Thus, I might have a quite productive afternoon fishing the pool, and never get the *just right* drift up under the travertine ledge that's needed to interest a fish there, because the runners upstream take often enough that I don't have a chance to concentrate on the spot under the ledge.

The spot under the ledge is the hardest in the pool to put a good drift through, but despite the grasping, weedy rock that lines it, it does not claim the most flies. This distinction belongs to the last spot, an area under the current tongue with a bottom comprised of a pile of boulders. Along with the hard current tongue providing overhead cover, these boulders are what make the spot so good. The browns all hold within a foot or two of the current line, over a distance of five or six feet upstream and down. By far the most productive line I've found is about a foot inside of the hardest pulse of current. When cast almost to the top of the pool along this line, drifted with a foot or two of slack in the fly line and a nine-foot leader tapered to 3X, flies are scraping bottom by the time they reach the sweet spot. About one time in ten this happens, they catch one of the rocks. Most of the time I get them back. Sometimes I don't.

It's usually easy to tell a fish from a snag in the spot among the rocks. Under the ledge it's not easy, but among the rocks a take is usually represented by one's indicator jerking a foot upstream and diving with authority. At times the first strike doesn't come until I've made fifty drifts with the same pair of nymphs, but when it does, the fish all-but hooks itself. Then it's off to the races; while fish hooked elsewhere in the pool tend to take a moment before running or jumping, perhaps "confused" in some sense of the word, due to the complicated currents and cover surrounding their lies, fish hooked near the current line bolt immediately, jumping and thrashing and hurtling downriver. I've lost perhaps six large runners that got way downstream on me, fish that got into the fast water below the pool, far more than I've landed, once they get that far downriver. All were hooked from this last spot.

•

August is perhaps the month in which I carry the most eclectic range of flies, ranging from big Chubby Chernobyls to match the Midnight Stoneflies that still hatch occasionally on the Yellowstone and Gardner to various Blue-winged Olive patterns to imitate the fall *Baetis* that start hatching between Gardiner and the head of Yankee Jim canyon on cold, wet days late in the month, in preparation for the dense hatches of September and October. Many days, it's a struggle to determine which flies to carry. I never struggle when

I set off to fish the ledge pool, however, and in fact often carry only two or three fly boxes. Only a still-thriving (if often subconscious) need to look the part of crazed fly fisherman keeps me carrying even this many flies, as well as more than two spools of tippet material. In the ledge pool, three patterns account for eighty percent of my fish, and I virtually always fish a 3X tippet with a 4X dropper.

All three fly patterns are big, generic nymphs. Probably my single most important fly in the ledge pool is a #12 Minch's Bead, Hare, and Copper, which always serves as a dropper to something else. While this is a fat-bodied nymph and larger than many anglers who visit in August would think to use, it is far smaller than the large nymphs many authorities advocate using for fall-run browns. Thus it is somewhat surprising that this is probably the fly on which I catch the most runners, whether in the ledge pool, the other deep pools the browns hold in consistently, or the fast, foamy pockets where they take refuge briefly as they move upstream.

I most often pair this fly with a #6 Brown Girdle Bug, probably the most consistent large nymph in the Rockies over the past few seasons. This one is a relatively new addition to the box. It produces far fewer fish than the Hare & Copper, but those it does produce are bigger and take harder than those that eat the smaller nymph. Moreover it's both large and heavy, while also not bulky, so it sinks like a brick, taking the Hare & Copper with it.

The third fly of the triumvirate is really the only one that really fits the mold of what people picture when they think of runner flies. It's a black flashback stonefly nymph with a black beadhead, tied in #4 by the Asian ladies employed by Dan Bailey's in far-off countries, which I grab from the Parks' Fly Shop bins when I head out the door after work, and in #2 by me, with an extra pair of rubber legs and a conehead instead of the bead. Even without my modifications, which are designed to make it even more irksome to the browns, it's hard to imagine a stonefly pattern that looks less like a stonefly nymph than this one.

Real stoneflies do not flash, at least not with the streaks of pearl flash that shoot from the back of this pattern. Real stoneflies do not have slim, smooth bodies of black dubbing or yarn. Real stoneflies do not have dense, oversized brown hackles at their heads, which pulse enough to make the fly a decent streamer, in a pinch. While I always carry Girdle Bugs and Hare & Coppers, even when I'm not fishing for runners, I always carry them, in prominent compartments of my go-to nymph box. When I'm fishing for anything except runner browns, the flashback stones usually stay in the car. Even in the few instances when I've used them elsewhere, I don't think they've produced a single fish. They just look wrong, if their intended purpose is imitative. As irritators, they excel. While the Girdle Bug and Bead, Hare, and Copper probably beat out the flashback stone in numbers of fish, the most vicious strikes seem to come to the flashback. All of the truly large runners I've ever hooked, fish over twenty-three inches, have taken this fly. I've seen it glaring from their mouths when they leap and tailwalk, and have had to duck to avoid it when it comes flying back at me when these monsters get off, as they have always done.

I still hope.

•

August and the first two weeks of September make up the ledge pool's prime season. I have caught one runner in July, a mile above the pool, but this was in 2001, a drought year, when the low water in the Yellowstone and perhaps some thought of cold water in the Gardner above Boiling River brought a few fish up early. It was impossible to mistake this fish as a resident. Its flanks were silver, with scarcely a hint of yellow, its back was purple and its spots few and scattered. Like most of the brown trout from the Yellowstone, it showed its Loch Leven heritage, this early in the run, its genes giving it coloration and heft more suited to a trout that spent most of the year in the icy North Atlantic. All the runners look like this. But I have never hooked such a fish in the ledge pool before August, though I have tried. In July, the pool is still buried by whitewater coursing down from the narrow slot above, making it impossible to get flies down to the bottom. Fish certainly live there, including the earliest handful of runners, and the residents must have a veritable smorgasbord to sample. The runners, which do not eat save out of aggression, as befits their anadromous heritage, find shelter beneath the frothy rush overhead, and are safe from angler and osprey, and the bald eagles that nest nearby.

During the first week of August, the pockets at the top of the pool come into shape. Strikes here are hard, as the pockets are small and shallower than the rest of the pool, so when a fish decides to strike, it must do so immediately, with great force. The closest I have come to having my rod jerked from my hands by a fish was when a fish took a #2 stonefly nymph in one of these pockets. It was small for a runner, fifteen inches, but bright and football-shaped, and it fought long and desperately.

The lower spots, the sweet spot under the current tongue and the slightly-less-sweet spot under the ledge, are not yet at their best this early, but they can fish. They require shot, sometimes as many as three tin BB shot, and heavily-weighted flies, and even then the cast must be perfect, just inside the current tongue, which is still swift enough to carry any rig downstream to the ledge and beyond, into the tailout of the pool, without the bugs getting deep enough to interest any but the most eager runners if the cast and drift are just a bit off. Some of my most surprising fish come at this season. Local wisdom has it that the larger runners, fish over twenty inches, do not begin to ascend until late September at the earliest, but I have hooked several of twenty to twenty-four inches from the pool before Labor Day, though I've never landed one over twenty-two.

By perhaps the fifteenth or twentieth, the pool is in prime shape, and remains so until sometime between Labor Day and September 20, depending on how high the winter snowpack was and how much summer rains keep the river's flows up. By now the river has dropped enough so that even the current tongue is not so violent that it prevents flies from getting down, and the depth of the pool itself is now less. At this season the Gardner flows at perhaps half the volume it carried in late July, so that at times the flashing of whitefish and fresh browns becomes visible. Standing on the hillside above, always after I'm done fishing since the shadows so cast completely cover the pool, the shadows of trout and whitefish and then the fish themselves materialize from what had

169

seemed a rocky-bottomed but otherwise empty pool, from streamside.

These are the pool's glory days. Every inch of it is now fishable, and with the first cool days that show summer is beginning to crack, browns begin ascending the river in earnest. These early fish almost all ascend high into the Gardner to spawn, well above Boiling River, and thus all must pass through the Ledge Pool at one time or another. If the proper flies pass down the pool at the proper depth, and are kept out of the rocks beneath the current tongue or from the grasping weed on the travertine ledge, odds are that at least one brown will find them of interest, over the course of an afternoon. Of course, this is also when it is most difficult to keep one's flies from becoming snared, as shot are still needed to get flies down, but if one's indicator is not placed at the proper depth and if one's drift is not perfect, these shot will carry the flies down too soon and wrap around the two largest boulders in the gut of the run. I have lost perhaps a hundred flies to these rocks. On a bad day two years ago, a day with few runners but many snags, I lost a dozen flies to them.

The increase in lost flies is largely a symptom of the decreasing power of the current tongue, and as such is a sign that this year's glory days fishing the ledge pool will soon come to an end. The current tongue provides cover and also serves as a deterrent to further upstream migration, meaning runner browns both have an incentive to rest once they reach the pool after their run through a long stretch of featureless pocket water and good water in which to do so, before facing more featureless pocket water upstream. As the tongue loses strength, through

September, the broken water from the force of the tongue's passage flattens, as does its overall velocity. Thus, runners can move onward more easily and also lack any incentive to remain and rest, since their pool is now exposed. The pockets at the head may hold fish slightly longer, but the rocks that form them, that had before been slightly submerged, are now exposed. Thus, though the pockets remain, they now lack surface cover as well. They are also shallow now, less than a foot deep in some places, meaning that if a fish holds in them, they probably do so at night.

No later than the end of September, not only is the pool no longer the perfect holding water it had been a month earlier, but there are fewer fish to hold in it. The lower Gardner is now no longer sweltering beneath the dual onslaught of the summer sun and the hot spring discharge from Boiling River, while the upper river begins to swiftly cool with the arrival of fall. It may snow at any time after Labor Day, and frosts fall most nights, and not just at high elevations. Thus the browns that begin to arrive in late September increasingly stay downstream, below or only a few pools above Boiling River, where the river is warmer. The latest, largest spawners, those that arrive in October or even November, a few weeks to either side of the end of the Park season, almost universally spawn below Boiling River. I know much about the ledge pool, but I do not know where the browns that fill it in August and early September go. Perhaps they ascend Lava Creek, perhaps they pair up and find what gravel they can here and there in the pocket water upstream of the ledge pool in the Gardner itself. Perhaps they gather in masses below

Osprey Falls, far up the inaccessible Sheepeater Canyon. I suspect they will always remain a mystery to me. That's not necessarily a bad thing.

•

The latest I have fished the ledge pool was in the middle of October. I had started far downstream, below Boiling River, and had taken runner after runner in every likely spot all the way to a pool about half a mile above Boiling River. Then I jumped far upriver to a cliff pool, the last good pool below the ledge pool, but one that's too shallow to often support runners. The sun was already hidden behind Sepulcher Peak, though it was only late afternoon, and in the flat light I took three more browns from the cliff pool. All were Gardner-resident browns in the 12-15" range, so richly-colored with their imminent spawn so as to seem a different species than the silvery-bright fish that ascend from the Yellowstone in August, fish two months from spawning, and still more richly-colored than the runners even now. After taking these three lovely fish, satisfied but curious, I hurried up to the ledge pool.

I fished almost exclusively for browns that fall, save for a few fabulous streamer days on the Yellowstone and a last attempt at Soda Butte, where all I caught were two lonely, cold cutts eating midges in a driving snowstorm, but since the fifteenth of September I had not visited the ledge pool. When I got there I was surprised to see it was a pool no longer. Instead it was two, the river having by now dropped so much that the lip of the travertine ledge broke the water's surface across much of the river's width, creating a current tongue where before there was none, a new tailout for a pool that in July was twice as